Personal Identity

Great Debates in Philosophy

Personal Identity
Sydney Shoemaker and Richard Swinburne

Consciousness and Causality
D. M. Armstrong and Norman Malcolm

Personal Identity

*Sydney Shoemaker
and Richard Swinburne*

Basil Blackwell

© Sydney Shoemaker and Richard Swinburne 1984

First published 1984
Basil Blackwell Publisher Limited
108 Cowley Road, Oxford OX4 1JF, England

British Library Cataloguing in Publication Data
Shoemaker, Sydney
    Personal identity.—(Great debates in philosophy)
    I. Identity
    I. Title   II. Swinburne, Richard
    III. Series
    ISBN 0–631–13208–2
    ISBN 0–631–13432–8 Pbk

Typeset at The Spartan Press Ltd, Lymington, Hants.

Contents

Great Debates in Philosophy

Since the time of Socrates, dialogue has been a powerful means of philosophical exploration and exposition. By presenting important current issues in philosophy in the form of a debate, this new series attempts to capture the flavour of philosophical argument and to convey the excitement generated by the exchange of ideas.

There will normally be more than two sides to any argument, and for any two 'opponents' there will be points of agreement as well as points of disagreement. The debate will not, therefore, necessarily cover every aspect of the chosen topic, nor will it present artificially polarized arguments. The aim is to provide, in a thought-provoking format, a series of clear accessible and concise introductions to a variety of subjects, ranging from formal logic to contemporary ethical issues. The series will be of interest to scholars, students and general readers alike, since each book brings together two outstanding philosophers to throw light on a topic of current controversy.

Each author contributes a major original essay stating his or her position. When these essays have been exchanged, the authors are each given the opportunity to respond to the opposing view. If the resulting book gives rise in its turn to further discussion, argument and debate among its readers it will have achieved its purpose.

Personal Identity
The Dualist Theory

RICHARD SWINBURNE

Acknowledgements

Earlier versions of some or all of this essay have been given as lectures or seminar papers in many different places—most recently in three seminars at the University of Adelaide in September 1982, in three lectures at University College, Cardiff in February 1983, and in three lectures in my series of Gifford Lectures at the University of Aberdeen in the Spring Term of 1983. I am most grateful for the helpful criticisms and generous hospitality which I received on all these occasions. My original paper on personal identity, which formed the basis of all my subsequent thinking on the subject was 'Personal Identity', *Proceedings of the Aristotelian Society*, 74 (1973–74), pp. 231–48. Much of the material of the present essay will be included in a much larger book, based on two series of Gifford Lectures, on 'Man'.

1 Empiricist Theories

There are two philosophical questions about personal identity. The first is: what are the logically necessary and sufficient conditions for a person P_2 at a time t_2 being the same person as a person P_1 at an earlier time t_1,[1] or, loosely, what does it mean to say that P_2 is the same person as P_1? The second is: what evidence of observation and experience can we have that a person P_2 at t_2 is the same person as a person P_1 at t_1 (and how are different pieces of evidence to be weighed against each other)? Many writers about personal identity have, however, needed to give only one account of personal identity, because their account of the logically necessary and sufficient conditions of personal identity was in terms of the evidence of observation and experience which would establish or oppose claims of personal identity. They have made no sharp distinction between the meaning of such claims and the evidence which supported them. Theories of this kind we may call empiricist theories.

In this section I shall briefly survey the empiricist theories which have been offered and argue that they are ultimately unsatisfactory, and so go on to argue that my two questions have very different answers. What we mean when we say that two persons are the same is one thing; the evidence which we may have to support our claim is something very different.

The most natural theory of personal identity which readily occurs to people, is that personal identity is constituted by bodily identity. P_2 is the same person as P_1 if P_2's body is the same body as P_1's body. The person to whom you are talking now and call 'John' is the same person as the person to whom you were talking last week and then called 'John' if and only if he has the same body. To say that the two bodies—call them B_1 and B_2—are the same is not to say that they contain exactly the same bits of matter. Bodies are continually taking in new

[1] The logically necessary and sufficient conditions for something being so are those conditions such that if they are present, that thing must be so; and if they are absent, that thing cannot be so—all this because of considerations of logic.

matter (by people eating and drinking and breathing in) and getting rid of matter. But what makes the bodies the same is that the replacement of matter is only gradual. The matter which forms my body is organized in a certain way, into parts— legs, arms, heart, liver, etc., which are interconnected and exchange matter and energy in regular ways. What makes my body today the same body as my body yesterday is that most of the matter is the same (although I may have lost some and gained some) and its organization has remained roughly the same.[2]

This bodily theory of personal identity gives a somewhat similar account of personal identity to the account which it is natural to give of the identity of any material object or plant, and which is due ultimately to Aristotle (*Metaphysics*, Bk 7). Aristotle distinguished between substances and properties. Substances are the individual things, like tables and chairs, cars and plants, which have properties (such as being square or round or red). Properties are 'universals', that is they can be possessed by many different substances; many different substances can be square or red. Substances are the individual substances which they are because of the matter out of which they are made and the form which is given to that matter. By 'the form' is meant those properties (normally of shape and organization), the possession of which is essential if a substance

[2]Some writers have attempted to analyse the notion of 'most of the matter' of yesterday's body being the same as 'most of the matter' of today's body in terms of today's body being composed largely of chunks of matter which are 'spatiotemporally continuous' with chunks of matter of yesterday's body, i.e., as linked to such chunks by a spatiotemporal chain. Two chunks of matter M_1 at time t_1 and M_2 at time t_2 are spatiotemporally continuous if and only if there is a material object M' identical in quantity and intrinsic properties to both M_1 and M_2 at every temporal instant t' between t_1 and t_2, such that each M' at each t' occupies a place contiguous with the place occupied by the M' at prior and succeeding instants of time if you take instants close enough in time to t'. (More precisely 'such that the place occupied by each M' at each t' is contiguous to places occupied by an M' at some instant t'' later than t' and all instants between t'' and t' and to places occupied by an M' at some instant t''' earlier than t' and all instants between t''' and t''.) It is very plausible to suppose that spatiotemporal continuity is a necessary condition for the identity of chunks of matter —chunks of matter cannot go from one place to another without moving along a path joining the places. But it is not so plausible to suppose that spatiotemporal continuity is a sufficient condition of the identity of chunks of matter, i.e., is enough to ensure that two chunks of matter are the same. It does not seem logically impossible that two qualitatively identical chunks should emerge from a given chunk. Something else than spatiotemporal continuity is needed to ensure that two chunks of matter are the same. On this, see Hirsch 1982, especially ch. 4.

is to be the substance in question, the properties which it cannot lose without ceasing to exist. We thus distinguish between the essential properties of a substance—those which constitute its form—and the accidental properties of a substance. It is among the essential properties of a certain oak tree that it has under normal conditions, a certain general shape and appearance, a certain life cycle (of producing leaves in spring and acorns in autumn); but its exact height, its position, and the distribution of leaves on its tallest branch are accidental properties. If the matter of the oak tree is reduced to a heap of planks, the oak tree, lacking its essential properties, has ceased to exist. We think of substances as belonging to different kinds, natural—e.g., oak trees or ferns; or artificial—e.g., cars or desks; and the defining properties of a kind constitute the form of a substance which belongs to it. Normally there is one and only one obvious kind to which we ascribe some given chunk of matter—a particular chunk of matter which we classify as an oak tree we would find it very unnatural to classify as belonging to any other kind—e.g., as a largely green thing more than twenty feet high. Although a substance may have the latter properties, it seems unnatural to think of them as forming a kind, and so of some substance being the substance it is because of its possession of those properties—with the consequence that it would cease to exist if the matter out of which it was made became brown instead. But sometimes a given chunk of matter may be thought of as belonging to one or other kind of thing—e.g., as a car or as a motor vehicle; and so we get a different substance according to the kind of thing we judge the matter to constitute. If the car is transformed into a lorry, the substance which was the car has ceased to exist, but the substance which was the motor vehicle has not.

What makes a substance the same substance as an earlier substance is that its matter is the same, or obtained from the matter of the former substance by gradual replacement, while continuing to possess the essential properties which constitute its form. The table at which I am writing today is the same table at which I was writing yesterday because it consists of the same matter (or at any rate, most of the same matter), organized in the same way—into the form of a table. For inanimate things, however, too much replacement of matter, however gradual, will destroy identity. If I replace the drawer of my desk by another drawer, the desk remains the same desk. But if, albeit gradually, I replace first the drawers and then the sides and then the top, so that there is none of the original matter left, we would say that the resulting desk was no longer the same desk as the original desk. For living things, such as plants, total replacement of matter—so long as it is gradual, and so long as physiology and anatomy also change only gradually if at all—will not destroy identity. The oak tree is the same as the sapling out of which it has grown, because replacement of matter has been gradual, and form (i.e., shape, physiology, and behaviour) has been largely preserved while any changes in it have been gradual.[3] This account of the identity of plants is also one which applies to social entities—such as a country or an army or a club. Two armies are the same, so long as any replacement of soldiers has been gradual and new soldiers play similar roles in the organization of the army to the roles played by those who have been replaced.

Persons too are substances. (Men, or human beings, are persons of a certain kind—viz., those with similar anatomy, physiology, and evolutionary origin to ourselves. There may be persons, e.g., on another planet, who are not human beings.) If we apply Aristotle's general account of the identity of substances to persons, it follows that for a person to be the same person as an earlier person, he has to have the same matter (or matter obtained from that earlier person by gradual replacement) organized into the form of person. The essential properties which make the form of a person would include, for Aristotle, not merely shape and physiological properties, but a kind of way of behaving and a capacity for a mental life of thought and feeling. For P_2 at t_2 to be the same person as P_1 at t_1, both have to be persons (to have a certain kind of body and mental life) and to be made of the same matter (i.e., to be such that P_2's body is obtained from P_1's by gradual replacement of parts). Such is the bodily theory of personal identity. It does not deny that persons have a mental life, but insists that what

---

[3]Aristotle did not himself go into the problem of how much matter has to continue the same if the substance is to be the same.

makes a person the same person as an earlier person is sameness of body.[4]

The difficulty which has been felt by those modern philosophers basically sympathetic to a bodily theory of personal identity is this. One part of the body—viz., the brain—seems to be of crucial importance for determining the characteristic behaviour of the rest. The brain controls not merely the physiology of the body but the way people behave and talk and think. If a man loses an arm or a leg, we do not think that the subsequent person is in any way different from the original person. If a man has a heart transplant or a liver transplant, again we do not think that the replacement makes a different person. On the other hand, if the brain of a person P_1 were removed from his body B_1 and transplanted into the skull of a body B_2 of a person P_2, from which the brain was removed and then transplanted into the empty skull of B_1 (i.e., if brains were interchanged), we would have serious doubt whether P_1 had any more the same body. We would be inclined to say that the person went where his brain went—viz., that P_1 at first had body B_1, and then, after the transplant, body B_2. The reason why we would say this is that (we have very good scientific reason to believe), the person with B_2's body would claim to be P_1, to have done and experienced the things which we know P_1 to have done, and would have the character, beliefs, and attitudes of P_1. What determines my attitude towards a person is not so much the matter out of which his body is made, but who he claims to be, whether he has knowledge of my past life purportedly on the basis of previous acquaintance with me, and more generally what his beliefs about the world are and what are his attitudes towards it. Hence a philosopher seeking a materialist criterion of personal identity, will come to regard the brain, the core of the body,

---

[4]Aristotle himself seemed to have some hesitation about the applicability of his theory of the identity of substances to the identity of persons. See, *De Anima* at 413a. He writes, first, 'that, therefore, the soul or certain parts of it, if it is divisible, cannot be separated from the body is quite clear'. But then he qualifies this by writing 'Not that anything prevents at any rate some parts from being separable'. He seems to be supposing that there are some capacities, e.g., for thought, which need no bodily material for their exercise. (For similar remarks see his 403a, 408b, 413b.) Aquinas develops these points into his doctrine that the Aristotle-type soul (the form of the body) is separable from the body. See below, pp. 31f for this doctrine and criticism of it.

rather than the rest of the body as what matters for personal identity. So this modified bodily theory states: that P_2 is the same person as P_1 if and only if P_2 has the same central organ controlling memory and character, viz., same brain, as P_1. Let us call it the brain theory of personal identity. A theory along these lines (with a crucial qualification, to be discussed shortly) was tentatively suggested by David Wiggins in *Identity and Spatiotemporal Continuity*.[5]

The traditional alternative to a bodily theory of personal identity is the memory-and-character theory. This claims that, given the importance for our attitude towards persons of their memory claims and character, continuity in respect of these would constitute personal identity—whether or not this continuity is caused by continuity of some bodily organ, such as the brain; and the absence of continuity of memory and character in some particular case involves the absence of personal identity, even if there is continuity in respect of that bodily organ which produces such continuity between other persons on other occasions.

The simplest version of this theory was that given by John Locke. According to Locke, memory alone, (or 'consciousness', as he often calls it) constitutes personal identity. Loosely—P_2 at t_2 is the same person as P_1 at an earlier time t_1, if and only if P_2 remembers having done and experienced various things, where these things were in fact done and experienced by P_1.[6]

Before expounding Locke's theory further we need to be clear about the kind of memory which is involved. First, it is what is sometimes called personal memory, i.e., memory of one's own past experiences. It is thus to be distinguished from factual memory, which is memory of some fact known previously; as when I remember that the battle of Hastings was

[5]Wiggins is even more tentative in the amended version of the book, *Sameness and Substance*.

[6]Although Locke's account of what it is for two persons to be the 'same person' is the simple memory account given above, he complicates it by providing a different account of what it is for two persons to be the 'same man'. This account is basically the bodily account which I have just outlined. P_1 is the same man as whoever has the same body as P_1, but the same person as whoever has the same memories as P_1. But Locke regards personal identity (which person, rather than which man, one is) as what is of importance for the way in which we should treat people, e.g., whom we are to reward or punish.

fought in 1066. This is not a memory of a past experience. Personal memory is also to be distinguished from remembering-how (e.g., to swim or to ride a bicycle), which is remembering how to perform some task. Secondly, it is personal memory in the weak sense. In the normal or strong sense of 'remember', one can only remember doing something if one really did it. I may say that I 'remember' going up the Eiffel Tower, but if I didn't do it, it seems natural to say that I cannot really remember having done it. In this sense, just as you can only know what is true, so you can only remember what you really did. However, there is also a weak sense of 'remember' in which a man remembers whatever he believes that he remembers in the strong sense. One's weak memories are not necessarily true ones. Now if the memory criterion defined personal identity in terms of memory in the strong sense, it would not be very useful; for to say that P_2 remembers having done what P_1 did would already entail their being the same person, and anyone in doubt as to whether P_2 was the same person as P_1, would have equal doubt whether P_2 really did remember doing what P_1 did. What the criterion as stated is concerned with is memory in the weak sense, which (because the strong sense is the more natural one) I shall henceforward call apparent memory.

So Locke's theory can now be rephrased as follows: P_2 at t_2 is the same person as P_1 at an earlier time t_1, if and only if P_2 apparently remembers having done and experienced various things when those things were in fact done and experienced by P_1. A person is who he thinks that he is. Note that what a person believes about his identity may be different from what he claims publicly. We only take public memory claims to be evidence of personal identity when we believe them to be honest, to express genuine memory beliefs, i.e., in my stated sense apparent memories. No doubt it is normally right to suppose that memory claims express apparent memories. But there may be circumstances in which it is reasonable to doubt this; e.g., if the subject has a source other than memory of the information which he claims to remember, if it is to his interest to pretend to remember, and if he is known to be deceitful.

Locke is very clear about the nature and consequences of his theory. If I do not apparently remember having done something, then I am not the same person as the person who did it. And if I do apparently remember having done the deeds of some person long since dead, then it follows that I am that person.

> If Socrates and the present mayor of Queenborough agree in [identity of consciousness], they are the same person: if the same Socrates waking and sleeping does not partake of the same consciousness, Socrates waking and sleeping is not the same person. And to punish Socrates waking for what sleeping Socrates thought, and waking Socrates was never conscious of, would be no more right, than to punish one twin for what his brother twin did, whereof he knew nothing. (Locke, *Essay*, sec. 19)

Locke's theory needs tidying up if we are to avoid absurdity. Consider, first, the following objection made by Thomas Reid:

> Suppose a brave officer to have been flogged when a boy at school for robbing an orchard, to have taken a standard from the enemy in his first campaign, and to have been made a general in advanced life; suppose also, which must be admitted to be possible, that, when he took the standard, he was conscious of his having been flogged at school, and that, when made a general, he was conscious of his taking the standard, but had absolutely lost the consciousness of his flogging. These things being supposed, it follows, from Mr Locke's doctrine, that he who was flogged at school is the same person who took the standard, and that he who took the standard is the same person who was made a general. Whence it follows if there be any truth in logic, that the general is the same person with him who was flogged at school. But the general's consciousness does not reach so far back as his flogging; therefore according to Mr Locke's doctrine, he is not the same person who was flogged. Therefore the general is, and at the same time is not, the same person with him who was flogged at school. (Reid, *Essays* III, ch. 6)

The objection illustrates the important point that identity is a transitive relation; if a is identical with b and b is identical with c, then necessarily a is identical with c. We can meet the objection by reformulating Locke's theory as follows: P_2 at t_2 is the same person as P_1 at an earlier time t_1 if and only if *either* P_2 apparently remembers what P_1 did and experienced, or he apparently remembers what some person P' at an intermediate time t' did and experienced, when

P' apparently remembers what P_1 did and experienced, *or* they are linked by some longer intermediate chain. (That is, P_2 apparently remembers what P' did and experienced, P' apparently remembers what P'' did and experienced, and so on until we reach a person who apparently remembers what P_1 did and experienced.) If P_1 and P_2 are linked by such a chain, they are, we may say, linked by continuity of memory. Clearly, the apparent memories of the deeds and experiences of the previous person at each stage in the chain need not be completely accurate memories of what was done and experienced. But they do need to be fairly accurate memories of what was done and experienced, if the later person is to be the person who did and experienced those things.

Secondly, Locke ought to allow that while in general apparent memory guarantees personal identity and so amounts to genuine memory, there are cases where it does not. One kind of case is one to which in effect I have just referred. If a person apparently remembers being the person who did or experienced a certain thing, that apparent memory is not genuine if no one did or experienced that thing. My apparent memory of having led a victorious army against the Russians in battle in 1976 is not genuine if no one did this deed. Also, an apparent memory is not genuine if it is caused by a chain of causes which runs outside the person (e.g., it is caused by some informant). If my apparent memory of having met my great-grandfather at the age of three months was caused by my mother telling me much later in life that I had done this thing, and my having forgotten that she was the sole source of my belief that I had met my great-grandfather, then my apparent memory is not genuine. Finally, if apparent memories are inconsistent (e.g., I apparently remember being in Australia at a certain time and I also apparently remember being in England at exactly that same time), then at least one of them cannot be genuine. Locke can allow that there are these exceptions, and that if any of them are found to hold we cannot regard an apparent memory as genuine, while insisting that, but for them, apparent memory guarantees personal identity.

Locke's memory theory was a simple theory, and a more complicated version of the theory which takes in other connected points was developed by Hume.[7] It is not only his apparent memory which determines the attitude which others have towards a person. How others treat a person depends also on his beliefs about the world and his attitudes towards it, whether they are changeable or constant, and what leads them to change—that is, on the person's character. Hume brings these in. He is also aware that if memory is not mistaken (and he assumes it normally to be correct), it is a causal relation. If in the strong sense I remember some past experience, this involves my past experience being in part the cause of my having the apparent memory which I do.

Hume regards a person as basically a mental state with a body attached; but the mental state is just a 'bundle or collection of different perceptions', i.e., of thoughts, sensations, and images. Some of these are caused by past 'perceptions' and among these are memories, which for Hume are faint copies of past 'perceptions'. The bundle of 'perceptions' C_2, which is my mental state now, is linked to the bundle of perceptions C_1, which we call my mental state yesterday, by the fact that some members of C_2 are caused by and resemble (e.g., include memories of and similar thoughts to) members of C_1, or are linked by a causal chain which passes through similar bundles. (Hume does not say what links 'perceptions' into one bundle—i.e., what makes all the 'perceptions' which I have at one time all mine.) Hume calls that kind of identity 'fictitious', because the 'perceptions' which belong to some bundle are really distinct entities from the 'perceptions' which belong to some other bundle, although linked causally to them; he contrasts it with the real identity which would be possessed by a substance which continued to exist in a perfectly unchanged state.

A number of more recent writers have developed more careful versions of a memory theory of personal identity, including Grice (1941) and Quinton (1962).

Many advocates of a memory theory have not always been very clear in their exposition about whether the apparent memories which form the links in the chain of memory need to

---

[7]Hume subsequently found this view outlined above and expanded in the main text of the *Treatise* unsatisfactory, as he wrote in his Appendix. But the grounds of his dissatisfaction are not clear. See Stroud 1977, ch. 6.

be actual memories, or whether they need only to be hypothetical memories. By 'actual memories' I mean actual recallings of past experiences. The trouble with the suggestion that actual memories are required is that we do not very often recall our past, and it seems natural to suppose that the deeds and experiences of some moments of a person's life never get recalled. Yet the memory theory, as stated so far, rules out that possibility. If I am not connected by a chain of memories with the deeds and experiences done by a person at a certain time, then I am not identical with that person. It is perhaps better if the theory claims that the apparent memories which form the links need only be hypothetical memories—i.e., what a person would apparently remember if he were to try to remember the deeds and experiences in question, e.g., in consequence of being prompted.[8]

There is however a major objection to any memory theory of personal identity, arising from the possibility of duplication. The objection was made briefly by Reid and at greater length in an influential article by Bernard Williams (1956–57). Williams imagines the case of a man whom he calls Charles who turns up in the twentieth century claiming to be Guy Fawkes:

> All the events he claims to have witnessed and all the actions he claims to have done point unanimously to the life-history of some one person in the past—for instance Guy Fawkes. Not only do all Charles' memory-claims that can be checked fit the pattern of Fawkes' life as known to historians, but others that cannot be checked are plausible, provide explanations of unexplained facts, and so on. (Williams, 1956–57, p. 332)

The fact that memory claims which 'cannot be checked are plausible, provide explanations of unexplained facts, and so on' is evidence that Charles is not merely claiming to remember

[8]We would need some well-justified theory by means of which we could infer what some person would apparently remember if he were to try, if we were ever to apply our theory to answering particular questions of the form 'Is P_2 identical with P_1?' The theory would need to be established without presupposing which past person, some person who is not now currently recalling anything, was. For although it is reasonable to suppose that such a person would remember many of his recent deeds and experiences, if he were to try, we cannot know which recent deeds and experiences were his until we know what he would apparently remember, according to the memory theory.

what he has in fact read in a book about Guy Fawkes, and so leaves us back with the supposition, natural to make in normal cases, that he is reporting honestly his apparent memories. So, by a memory theory Charles would be Guy Fawkes. But then suppose, Williams imagines, that another man Robert turns up, who satisfies the memory criteria for being Guy Fawkes equally well. We cannot say that they are both identical with Guy Fawkes, for if they were, they would be identical with each other—which they are not since they currently live different lives and have different thoughts and feelings from each other. So apparent memory cannot constitute personal identity, although it may be fallible evidence of it.

The objection from the possibility of duplication, together with other difficulties which will be mentioned in later chapters, have inclined the majority of contemporary writers to favour a theory which makes some sort of bodily continuity central to personal identity. As we have seen, the brain theory takes into account the insight of memory-and-character theory into the importance of these factors for personal identity, by selecting the brain, as the organ causally responsible for the continuity of memory and character, as that part of the body, the continuity of which constitutes the continuity of the person.

The trouble is that any brain theory is also open to the duplication objection. The human brain has two very similar hemispheres—a left and a right hemisphere. The left hemisphere plays a major role in the control of limbs of and processing of sensory information from the right side of the body (and from the right sides of the two eyes); and the right hemisphere plays a major role in the control of limbs of and processing of sensory information from the left side of the body (and from the left sides of the two eyes). The left hemisphere plays a major role in the control of speech. Although the hemispheres have different roles in the adult, they interact with each other; and if parts of a hemisphere are removed, at any rate early in life, the roles of those parts are often taken over by parts of the other hemisphere. Brain operations which remove substantial parts of the brain are not infrequent. It might be possible one day to remove a whole hemisphere, without killing the person. There are no logical difficulties in supposing that we could transplant one of P_1's hemispheres into one skull from which a brain had been removed, and the other hemisphere into another such skull, and that both transplants should take, and it may well be practically possible to do so. It is certainly more likely to occur than the Guy Fawkes story told by Williams! If these transplants took, clearly each of the resulting persons would behave to some extent like P_1, and indeed both would probably have some of the apparent memories of P_1. Each of the resulting persons would then be good candidates for being P_1.

After all, if one of P_1's hemispheres had been destroyed and the other remained intact and untransplanted, and the resulting person continued to behave and make memory claims some-what like those of P_1, we would have had little hesitation in declaring that person to be P_1. The same applies, whichever hemisphere was preserved—although it may well be that the resulting person would have greater capacities (e.g., speech) if one hemisphere was preserved than if the other one was preserved. We have seen earlier good reason for supposing that the person goes where his brain goes, and if his brain consists only of one hemisphere, that should make no difference. So if the one remaining hemisphere is then transplanted, we ought to say that the person whose body it now controls is P_1. Whether that person is P_1 can hardly be affected by the fact that instead of being destroyed, the other hemisphere is also transplanted so as to constitute the brain of a person. But if it is, that other person will be just as good a candidate for being P_1. So a Wiggins-type account might lead us to say that both resulting persons are P_1. But, for the reason given earlier in connection with the Guy Fawkes examples, that cannot be—since the two later persons are not identical with each other. Hence, Wiggins adds to his tentative definition a clause stating that P_2 who satisfies his criterion stated earlier is the same person as P_1, only if there is no other later person who also satisfies the criterion.[9]

But the introduction into any theory, whether a memory theory, a brain theory, or whatever, of a clause stating that a person who satisfies the criterion in question for being the same

[9]He suggests analysing 'person' in such a way that 'coincidence under the concept person logically required the continuance in one organized parcel of all that was causally sufficient and causally necessary to the continuance of essential and characteristic functioning, no autonomously sufficient part achieving autonomous and functionally separate existence' (Wiggins 1967, p. 55).

as an earlier person is the same, only so long as there is no other person who satisfies the criterion also or equally well, does have an absurd consequence. Let us illustrate this for the brain theory. Suppose P_1's left hemisphere is transplanted into some skull and the transplant takes. Then, according to the theory, whether the resulting person is P_1, i.e., whether P_1 survives, will depend on whether the other transplant takes. If it does, since both resulting persons will satisfy the memory and brain continuity criteria equally well, neither will be P_1. But if the other transplant does not take, then since there is only one person who satisfies the criterion, that person is P_1. So whether I survive an operation will depend on what happens in a body entirely different from the body which will be mine, if I do survive. But how can who I am depend on what happens to you? A similar absurd consequence follows when a similar clause forbidding duplication is added to a memory theory.

Yet if we abandon the duplication clause, we are back with the original difficulty—that there may be more than one later person who satisfies any memory criterion or brain criterion, or combination thereof, for being the same person as an earlier person. Our discussion brings to our attention also the fact that both these criteria are criteria which may be satisfied to varying degrees. P_2 can have 90 per cent, or 80 per cent, or less than 50 per cent of the brain of P_1; and likewise the similarity of apparent memory and character may vary along a spectrum. Just how well do criteria have to be satisfied for the later person to be the same person as the earlier person? Any line one might draw seems totally artificial. One might think that it was non-arbitrary to insist on more than 50 per cent of the original brain matter—for only one later person could have more than 50 per cent of the original brain matter (whereas if our criterion demands only a smaller proportion, more than one later person could satisfy it). But would we really want to say that P_6 was the same person as P_1 if P_2 was obtained from P_1 by a transplant of 60 per cent (and so more than half) of P_1's brain matter, P_3 was obtained from P_2 by a transplant of 60 per cent of P_2's brain matter, and so on until we came to P_6. By the criterion of 'more than half of the brain matter', P_6 would be the same person as P_5, P_5 as P_4 and so on, and so by the transitivity of identity P_6 would be the same person as P_1—although he would have very little of P_1's brain matter. Any criterion of the proportion of brain matter transferred, to be plausible, would have to take account of whether there had been similar transplants in the past, and the length of the interval between them. And then the arbitrariness of the criterion would stare us in the face.

This problem pushes the thinker towards one of two solutions. The first solution is to say that personal identity is a matter of degree. P_2 is the same person as P_1 to the extent to which there is sameness of brain matter and continuity of memory. After all, survival for inanimate things is a matter of degree. As we gradually replace bits of a desk with new bits, the resulting desk is only more or less the same as the original desk. And if my car is taken to pieces and some of the bits are used to make one new car, and some of the bits used to make another new car, both cars are partly the same as and partly different from the old car. Why cannot we say the same of people? Normally we are not inclined to talk thus, because brain operations are rare and brain hemisphere transplants never happen. Hence there is normally at most only one candidate for being the same person as an earlier person, and he is normally a very strong candidate indeed—having a more or less identical brain and very great similarities of apparent memory and character. So we tend to think of personal identity as all or nothing. But it is not thus in its logic, the argument goes. There is the logical possibility, which could become an empirical possibility, of intermediate cases—of persons who are to some extent the same as and to some extent different from original persons.

This view has been advocated by Derek Parfit (1971b). When a person divides, as a result of a split brain transplant, he 'survives' in part, Parfit holds, as each of two persons. They constitute his later 'selves', neither of whom, to speak strictly, are identical with the original person.

This theory which Parfit calls the complex view,[10] does however, run up against a fundamental difficulty that it commits him to substantial empirical claims which to all appearance could very easily be false. I can bring this out by adopting Bernard Williams's famous mad surgeon story (in

[10]He introduces this terminology in his paper, Parfit 1971a.

Williams 1970). Suppose that a mad surgeon captures you and announces that he is going to transplant your left cerebral hemisphere into one body, and your right one into another. He is going to torture one of the resulting persons and free the other with a gift of a million pounds. You can choose which person is going to be tortured and which to be rewarded, and the surgeon promises to do as you choose. You believe his promise. But how are you to choose? You wish to choose that you are rewarded, but you do not know which resultant person will be you. Now on the complex theory each person will be you to the extent to which he has your brain and resembles you in his apparent memories and character. It would be in principle empirically ascertainable whether and to what extent persons with right hemisphere transplants resemble their originals in apparent memories and character more or less than persons with left hemisphere transplants. But clearly the difference is not going to be great. So Parfit must say that your choice does not greatly matter. Both subsequent persons will be in part you—although perhaps to slightly different degrees. And so you will —although perhaps to slightly different degrees—in part suffer and in part enjoy what each suffers and enjoys. So you have reason both for joyous expectation and for terrified anticipation. But one problem is: how could you have reason for part joyous expectation and part terrified anticipation, when no one future person is going to suffer a mixed fate?

But even if this notion of partial survival does make sense, the more serious difficulty remains, which is this. We can make sense of the supposition that the victim makes the wrong choice, and has the experience of being tortured and not the experience of being rewarded; or the right choice, and has the experience of being rewarded and not the experience of being tortured. A mere philosophical analysis of the concept of personal identity cannot tell you which experiences will be yours tomorrow. To use Bernard Williams's telling word, any choice would be a 'risk'. But on Parfit's view no risk would be involved—for knowing the extent of continuity of brain, apparent memory, and character, you would know the extent to which a future person would be you and so the extent to which his experiences would be yours. Although it *may* be the case that if my cerebral hemispheres are transplanted into different bodies, I survive partly as the person whose body is controlled by one and partly as the person whose body is controlled by the other, it may not be like that at all. Maybe I go where the left hemisphere goes; and when my right hemisphere is separated from the left hemisphere and comes to control a body by itself, either a new person is formed, or the resulting organism, although behaving to some extent like a person is really a very complicated non-conscious machine. As we have noted, the fate of some parts of my body, such as my arms and legs, is quite irrelevant to the fate of me. And plausibly the fate of some parts of my brain is irrelevant—can I not survive completely a minor brain operation which removes a very small tumour? But then maybe it is the same with some larger parts of the brain too. We just don't know. If the mad surgeon's victim took the attitude that it didn't matter which way he chose, we must, I suggest, regard him as taking an unjustifiably dogmatic attitude.

The alternative way out of the duplication problem is to say that although apparent memory and brain continuity are, as they obviously are, evidence of personal identity, they are fallible evidence and personal identity is something distinct from them. Just as the presence of blood stains and fingerprints matching those of a given man are evidence of his earlier presence at the scene of the crime, and the discovery of Roman-looking coins and buildings is evidence that the Romans lived in some region, so the similarity of P_2's apparent memory to that of P_1 and his having much the same brain matter, is evidence that P_2 is the same person as P_1. Yet blood stains and fingerprints are one thing and a man's earlier presence at the scene of the crime another. His presence at the scene of the crime is not analysable in terms of the later presence of blood stains and fingerprints. The latter is evidence of the former, because you seldom get blood stains and fingerprints at a place matching those of a given man, unless he has been there leaving them around. But it might happen. So, the suggestion is, personal identity is distinct from, although evidenced by, similarity of memory and continuity of brain.

This account, which for the moment I will follow Parfit in calling the simple view, can meet all the difficulties which have beset the other theories which we have discussed. The difficulty for the complex view was that it seemed very peculiar to suppose that mere logic could determine which of the experiences had by various persons, each of which was to some extent continuous with me in apparent memory and brain matter, would be mine. There seemed to be a further truth—that I would or would not have those experiences—beyond any truths about the extent of similarity in apparent memory and matter of future persons to myself. The simple view claims explicitly that personal identity is one thing, and the extent of similarity in matter and apparent memory another. There is no contradiction in supposing that the one should occur without the other. Strong similarity of matter and apparent memory is powerful evidence of personal identity. I and the person who had my body and brain last week have virtually the same brain matter and such similar apparent memory, that it is well-nigh certain that we are the same person. But where the brain matter is only in part the same and the memory connection less strong, it is only fairly probable that the persons are the same. Where there are two later persons P_2 and P_2^*, each of whom had some continuity with the earlier person P_1, the evidence supports to some extent each of the two hypotheses—that P_2 is the same person as P_1, and that P_2^* is the same person as P_1. It may give more support to one hypothesis than to the other, but the less well supported hypothesis might be the true one, or maybe neither hypothesis is true. Perhaps P_1 has ceased to exist, and two different persons have come into existence. So the simple view fully accepts that mere logic cannot determine which experiences will be mine, but it allows that continuity of apparent memory and brain provides fallible evidence about this. And of course the duplication objection that they allow for the two subsequent persons being the same person, which we brought against the brain and the memory theories, has no force against the simple theory. For although there can be equally good evidence that each of two later persons is the same person as an earlier person, that evidence is fallible; and since clearly only one person at one time can be strictly the same person as some person at an earlier time, it follows that in one case the evidence is misleading—although we may not know in which case.

There are, however, other difficulties with the simple view and to these I shall come in due course. In the next section I will expound and develop the simple view, and show that it amounts to the same as Cartesian dualism—the view that a person consists of two parts, soul, and body. In section 3 I shall attempt to rebut verificationist objections to the simple view, and argue that on the simple view the continuing existence of the person is something of which the subject is aware in his own experience. In section 4 I shall attempt to show, why, if personal identity is not constituted by continuity of brain and memory, the latter are nevertheless evidence of it.

The simple view is normally combined with the doctrine that persons are indivisible, in the sense that only one person P_2 at t_2 can be in any degree the same person as P_1 at t_1; and only one person P_1 at t_1 can in any degree be the same person as P_2 at t_2. Not merely is strict identity of one person with two distinct earlier persons or two distinct later persons impossible, but so is partial identity (e.g., Parfit-style 'survival'). Neither fission nor fusion of persons is possible. When a brain is split, at most one of any resulting persons is to any degree the same as the original person; and if hemispheres from separate brains are put together to form the brain of a new person, at most one of the original persons from whose brains the hemispheres were transplanted is to any degree the same as the later person, and any identity is full identity. We have so far noted briefly one argument in favour of the indivisibility thesis (p. 18)—the difficulty of giving any sense to the supposition that a person P_1 about to undergo fission will have in any degree the experiences of both of the two persons P_2 and P_2* who will in no way have shared each other's experiences. Two later cars or tables can be in part the same as and in part different from an earlier car or table; but cars and tables do not have experiences, and so this difficulty does not arise for them. We shall consider in due course a brief argument against the possibility of fusion, to back up the argument against fission, and so complete the defence of both parts of the indivisibility thesis, but note that although normally combined with the simple view, the indivisibility thesis can be separated from it. I have made that separation. As I shall understand it, the simple view is simply the view that the truth about personal identity is not analysable in terms of the fallible empirical evidence for it of brain and memory continuity; and my primary concern is with the simple view.

2 The Dualist Theory

The brain transplant considerations of the first section leading to the simple view of personal identity showed that significant continuity of brain and memory was not enough to ensure personal identity. They did not show that continuity of brain or memory were totally dispensable; that P_2 at time t_2 could be the same person as P_1 at an earlier time t_1, even though P_2 had none of the brain matter (or other bodily matter) of P_1 and had no apparent memory of P_1's actions and experiences. A number of more extravagant thought-experiments do, however, show that there is no contradiction in this latter supposition.

There seems no contradiction in the supposition that a person might acquire a totally new body (including a completely new brain)—as many religious accounts of life after death claim that men do. To say that this body, sitting at the desk in my room is my body is to say two things. First it is to say that I can move parts of this body (arms, legs, etc.), just like that, without having to do any other intentional action and that I can make a difference to other physical objects only by moving parts of this body. By holding the door handle and turning my hand, I open the door. By bending my leg and stretching it I kick the ball and make it move into the goal. But I do not turn my hand or bend my leg by doing some other intentional action; I just do these things.[11] Secondly, it is to say that my knowledge of states of the world outside this body is derived from their effects on this body—I learn about the positions of physical objects by seeing them, and seeing them involves light rays reflected by them impinging on my eyes and setting up nervous impulses in my optic nerve. My body is the vehicle of my agency in the world and my knowledge of the world. But then is it not coherent to suppose that I might suddenly find that my present body no longer served this function, that I could no longer acquire

[11]Following A. C. Danto (1965), philosophers call those intentional actions which we just do, not by doing some other intentional action, basic actions, and those which we do by doing some other intentional action, mediated actions. An intentional action is one which an agent does, meaning to do. No doubt certain events have to happen in our nerves and muscles if we are to move our arms and legs, but we do not move our arms and legs by intentionally making these events occur.

information through these eyes or move these limbs, but might discover that another body served the same function? I might find myself moving other limbs and acquiring information through other eyes. Then I would have a totally new body. If that body, like my last body, was an occupant of the Earth, then we would have a case of reincarnation, as Eastern religions have understood that. If that body was an occupant of some distant planet, or an environment which did not belong to the same space[12] as our world, then we would have a case of resurrection as on the whole Western religions (Christianity, Judaism and Islam) have understood that.

This suggestion of a man acquiring a new body (with brain) may be more plausible, to someone who has difficulty in grasping it, by supposing the event to occur gradually. Suppose that one morning a man wakes up to find himself unable to control the right side of his body, including his right arm and leg. When he tries to move the right-side parts of his body, he finds that the corresponding left-side parts of his body move; and when he tries to move the left-side parts, the corresponding right-side parts of his wife's body move. His knowledge of the world comes to depend on stimuli to his left side and to his wife's right side (e.g., light rays stimulating his left eye and his wife's right eye). The bodies fuse to some extent physiologically as with Siamese twins, while the man's wife loses control of her right side. The focus of the man's control of and knowledge of the world is shifting. One may suppose the process completed as the man's control is shifted to the wife's body, while the wife loses control of it.

Equally coherent, I suggest, is the supposition that a person might become disembodied. A person has a body if there is one particular chunk of matter through which he has to operate on and learn about the world. But suppose that he finds himself able to operate on and learn about the world within some small finite region, without having to use one particular chunk of matter for this purpose. He might find himself with knowledge of the position of objects in a room (perhaps by having visual

---

[12]Two objects belong to the same space if they are at some distance from each other, if you can get from one to the other by going along a path in space which joins them. For a fuller account of the meaning of the claim that an object occupies a different space from our space, see Swinburne 1981b, chs 1 and 2.

sensations, perhaps not), and able to move such objects just like that, in the ways in which we know about the positions of our limbs and can move them. But the room would not be, as it were, the person's body; for we may suppose that simply by choosing to do so he can gradually shift the focus of his knowledge and control, e.g., to the next room. The person would be in no way limited to operating and learning through one particular chunk of matter. Hence we may term him disembodied. The supposition that a person might become disembodied also seems coherent.

I have been arguing so far that it is coherent to suppose that a person could continue to exist with an entirely new body or with no body at all. (And I would also suggest by the way, though I shall deal more fully with this point in section 4, that in the cases cited the subject would in some circumstances have reason to believe, through his memory of what he had just experienced, that this had happened to him.) Could a person continue to exist without any apparent memory of his previous doings? Quite clearly, we do allow not merely the logical possibility, but the frequent actuality of amnesia—a person forgetting all or certain stretches of his past life. Despite Locke, many a person does forget much of what he has done. But, of course, we normally only suppose this to happen in cases where there is the normal bodily and brain continuity. Our grounds for supposing that a person forgets what he has done are that the evidence of bodily and brain continuity suggests that he was the previous person who did certain things, which he now cannot remember having done. And in the absence of both of the main kinds of evidence for personal identity, we would not be justified in supposing that personal identity held. (Character continuity is a minor kind of evidence, hardly of great importance on its own—as we shall see in section 4.) For that reason I cannot describe a case where we would have good reason to suppose that P_2 was identical with P_1, even though there was neither brain continuity nor memory continuity between them. However, only given verificationist dogma, is there any reason to suppose that the only things which are true are those of whose truth we can have evidence, and I shall suggest in section 3 that there is no good reason for believing verificationism to be true. We can make sense of states of affairs being true, of which we can have no evidence that they are true. And among them surely is the supposition that the person who acquires another body loses not merely control of the old one, but memories of what he did with its aid. Again, many religions have taken seriously stories of persons passing through the waters of Lethe (a river whose waters made a person forget all his previous life) and then acquiring a new body. Others who have heard these stories may not have believed them true; but they have usually claimed to understand them, and (unless influenced by philosophical dogma) have not suspected them of involving contradiction.

Those who hope to survive their death, despite the destruction of their body, will not necessarily be disturbed if they come to believe that they will then have no memory of their past life on Earth; they may just want to survive and have no interest in continuing to recall life on Earth. Again, apparently, there seems to be no contradiction involved in their belief. It seems to be a coherent belief (whether or not true or justified). Admittedly, there may be stories or beliefs which involve a hidden contradiction when initially they do not seem to do so. But the fact that there seems (and to so many people) to be no contradiction hidden in these stories is good reason for supposing that there is no contradiction hidden in them—until a contradiction is revealed. If this were not a good reason for believing there to be no contradiction, we would have no good reason for believing any sentence at all to be free of hidden contradiction.

Not merely is it not logically necessary that a person have a body made of certain matter, or have certain apparent memories, if he is to be the person which he is; it is not even necessitated by laws of nature.[13] For let us assume that natural laws dictated the course of evolution and the emergence of consciousness. In 4000 million BC the Earth was a cooling globe of inanimate atoms. Natural laws then, we assume, dictated how this globe would evolve, and so which arrangements of matter will be the bodies of conscious men, and just how apparent memories of conscious men depend on their brain states. My point now is that what natural laws in no way determine is which animate body is yours and which is mine. Just the same arrangement of matter and just the same laws

[13] I owe this argument to Knox 1969.

could have given to me the body (and so the apparent memories) which are now yours, and to you the body (and so the apparent memories) which are now mine. It needs either God or chance to allocate bodies to persons; the most that natural laws determine is that bodies of a certain construction are the bodies of some person or other, who in consequence of this construction have certain apparent memories. Since the body which is presently yours (together with the associated apparent memories) could have been mine (logic and even natural laws allow), that shows that none of the matter of which my body is presently made (nor the apparent memories) is essential to my being the person I am. That must be determined by something else.

The view that personal identity is something ultimate, unanalysable in terms of such observable and experienceable phenomena as bodily continuity and continuity of memory, was put forward in the eighteenth century by Butler, and, slightly less explicitly, by Reid. In recent years R. M. Chisholm (1969) has put forward a similar view.

I could just leave my positive theory at that—that personal identity is unanalysable. But it will, I hope, be useful to express it in another way, to bring out more clearly what it involves and to connect it with another whole tradition of philosophical thought.

In section 1, I set out Aristotle's account of the identity of substances: that a substance at one time is the same substance as a substance at an earlier time if and only if the later substance has the same form as, and continuity of matter (in the sense delineated on p. 5) with, the earlier substance. On this view a person is the same person as an earlier person if he has the same form as the earlier person (i.e., both are persons) and has continuity of matter with him (i.e., has the same body).

Certainly, to be the same person as an earlier person, a later person has to have the same form—i.e., has to be a person. If my arguments for the logical possibility of there being disembodied persons are correct, then the essential characteristics of a person constitute a narrower set than those which Aristotle would have included. My arguments suggest that all that a person needs to be a person are certain mental capacities—for having conscious experiences (e.g., thoughts or sensations) and performing intentional actions. Thought-experiments of the kind described earlier allow that a person might lose his body, but they describe his continuing to have conscious experiences and his performing or being able to perform intentional actions, i.e., to do actions which he means to do, bring about effects for some purpose.

Yet if my arguments are correct, showing that two persons can be the same, even if there is no continuity between their bodily matter, we must say that in the form stated the Aristotelian account of identity applies only to inanimate objects and plants and has no application to personal identity.[14] We are then faced with a choice either of saying that the criteria of personal identity are different from those for other substances, or of trying to give a more general account than Aristotle's of the identity of substances which would cover both persons and other substances. It is possible to widen the Aristotelian account so that we can do the latter. We have only to say that two substances are the same if and only if they have the same form and there is continuity of the stuff of which they are made, and allow that there may be kinds of stuff other than matter. I will call this account of substance identity the wider Aristotelian account. We may say that there is a stuff of another kind, immaterial stuff, and that persons are made of both normal bodily matter and of this immaterial stuff but that it is the continuity of the latter which provides that continuity of stuff which is necessary for the identity of the person over time.

This is in essence the way of expressing the simple theory which is adopted by those who say that a person living on Earth consists of two parts—a material part, the body; and an immaterial part, the soul. The soul is the essential part of a person, and it is its continuing which constitutes the continuing of the person. While on Earth, the soul is linked to a body (by the body being the vehicle of the person's knowledge of and action upon the physical world). But, it is logically possible, the soul can be separated from the body and exist in a disembodied state (in the way described earlier) or linked to a new body. This way of expressing things has been used in many religious

---

[14]I do not discuss the difficult issue of whether the Aristotelian account applies to animals other than man, e.g., whether continuity of matter and form is necessary and sufficient for the identity of a dog at a later time with a dog at an earlier time.

traditions down the centuries, for it is a very natural way of expressing what is involved in being a person once you allow that a person can survive the death of his body. Classical philosophical statements of it are to be found in Plato and, above all, in Descartes. I shall call this view classical dualism.

I wrote that 'in essence' classical dualism is the view that there is more stuff to the person than bodily matter, and that it is the continuing of this stuff which is necessary for the continuing of the person, because a writer such as Descartes did not distinguish between the immaterial stuff, let us call it soul-stuff, and that stuff being organized (with or without a body) as one soul. Descartes and other classical dualists however did not make this distinction, because they assumed (implicitly) that it was not logically possible that persons divide—i.e., that an earlier person could be in part the same person as each of two later persons. Hence they implicitly assumed that soul-stuff comes in essentially indivisible units. That is indeed what one has to say about soul-stuff, if one makes the supposition (as I was inclined to do, in section 1), that it is not logically possible that persons divide. There is nothing odd about supposing that soul-stuff comes in essentially indivisible units. Of any chunk of matter, however small, it is always logically, if not physically, possible that it be divided into two. Yet it is because matter is extended, that one can always make sense of it being divided. For a chunk of matter necessarily takes up a finite volume of space. A finite volume of space necessarily is composed of two half-volumes. So it always makes sense to suppose that part of the chunk which occupies the left half-volume of space to be separated from that part of the chunk which occupies the right half-volume. But that kind of consideration has no application to immaterial stuff. There is no reason why there should not be a kind of immaterial stuff which necessarily is indivisible; and if the supposition of section 1 is correct, the soul-stuff will have that property.

So then—once we modify the Aristotelian understanding of the criteria for the identity of substances, the simple view of personal identity finds a natural expression in classical dualism. The arguments which Descartes gave in support of his account of persons are among the arguments which I have given in favour of the simple theory and since they take for granted the wider Aristotelian framework, they yield classical dualism as a consequence. Thus Descartes argues:

> Just because I know certainly that I exist, and that meanwhile I do not remark that any other thing necessarily pertains to my nature or essence, excepting that I am a thinking thing, I rightly conclude that my essence consists solely in the fact that I am a thinking thing. And although possibly . . . I possess a body with which I am very intimately conjoined, yet because, on the one side, I have a clear and distinct idea of myself inasmuch as I am only a thinking and unextended thing, and as, on the other, I possess a distinct idea of body, inasmuch as it is only an extended and unthinking thing, it is certain that this I [that is to say, my soul by which I am what I am], is entirely and absolutely distinct from my body, and can exist without it.[15]

Descartes is here saying that he can describe a thought-experiment in which he continues to exist although his body does not. I have also described such a thought-experiment and have argued, as Descartes in effect does, that it follows that his body is not logically necessary for his existence, that it is not an essential part of himself. Descartes can go on 'thinking' (i.e., being conscious) and so existing without it. Now if we take the wider Aristotelian framework for granted that the continuing of a substance involves the continuing of some of the stuff of which it is made, and since the continuing existence of Descartes does not involve the continuing of bodily matter, it follows that there must now be as part of Descartes some other stuff, which he calls his soul, which forms the essential part of Descartes.

Given that for any present person who is currently conscious, there is no logical impossibility, whatever else may be true now of that person, that that person continue to exist without his body, it follows that that person must now actually have a part other than a bodily part which can continue, and which we may call his soul—and so that his possession of it is entailed by his being a conscious thing. For there is not even a logical possibility that if I now consist of nothing but matter and the matter is destroyed, that I should nevertheless continue to

---

[15]Descartes, *Meditations*, p. 190. The clause in square brackets occurs only in the French translation, approved by Descartes.

exist. From the mere logical possibility of my continued existence there follows the actual fact that there is now more to me than my body; and that more is the essential part of myself. A person's being conscious is thus to be analysed as an immaterial core of himself, his soul being conscious.[16]

So Descartes argues, and his argument seems to me correct —given the wider Aristotelian framework. If we are prepared to say that substances can be the same, even though none of the stuff (in a wide sense) of which they are made is the same, the conclusion does not follow. The wider Aristotelian framework provides a partial definition of 'stuff' rather than a factual truth.

[16]It may be useful, in case anyone suspects the argument of this paragraph of committing some modal fallacy, to set it out in a more formal logical shape. I use the usual logical symbols—'.' means 'and', '∼' means 'not', '◇' means 'it is logically possible'. I then introduce the following definitions:

p = 'I am a conscious person, and I exist in 1984'
q = my body is destroyed at the end of 1984
r = I have a soul in 1984
s = I exist in 1985
x ranges over all consistent propositions compatible with (p. q) and describing 1984 states of affairs
('(x)' is to be read in the normal way as 'for all states x . . .')

The argument may now be set out as follows:

p	Premise (1)
$(x) \diamond (p.q.x.s)$	Premise (2)
$\sim \diamond (p.q.\sim r.s)$	Premise (3)

∴ ∼r is not within the range of x.

But since ∼r describes a state of affairs in 1984, it is not compatible with (p.q). But q can hardly make a difference to whether or not r. So p is incompatible with ∼r.

∴ r

The argument is designed to show that r follows from p; and so, more generally, that every conscious person has a soul. Premise (3) is justified by the wider Aristotelian principle that if I am to continue, some of the stuff out of which I am made has to continue. As I argued in the text, that stuff must be non-bodily stuff. The soul is defined as that non-bodily part whose continuing is essential for my continuing.

Premise (2) relies on the intuition that whatever else might be the case in 1984, compatible with (p.q), my stream of consciousness could continue thereafter.

If you deny (2) and say that r is a state of affairs not entailed by (p.q), but which has to hold if it is to be possible that s, you run into this difficulty. There may be two people in 1984, Oliver who has a soul, and Fagin, who does not. Both are embodied and conscious, and to all appearances indistinguishable. God (who can do all things logically possible, compatible with how the world is up to now), having forgotten to give Fagin a soul, has, as he annihilates Fagin's body at the end of 1984, no power to continue his stream of thought. Whereas he has the power to continue Oliver's stream of thought. This seems absurd.

To say that a person has an immaterial soul is not to say that if you examine him closely enough under an acute enough microscope you will find some very rarefied constituent which has eluded the power of ordinary microscopes. It is just a way of expressing the point within a traditional framework of thought that persons can—it is logically possible—continue, when their bodies do not. It does, however, seem a very natural way of expressing the point—especially once we allow that persons can become disembodied. Unless we adopt a wider Aristotelian framework, we shall have to say that there can be substances which are not made of anything, and which are the same substances as other substances which are made of matter.

It does not follow from all this that a person's body is no part of him. Given that what we are trying to do is to elucidate the nature of those entities which we normally call 'persons', we must say that arms and legs and all other parts of the living body are parts of the person. My arms and legs are parts of me. The crucial point that Descartes was making is that the body is only, contingently and possibly temporarily, part of the person; it is not an essential part. However, Descartes does seem in a muddle about this. In the passage from the *Meditations* just cited, as elsewhere in his works,[17] he claims sometimes (wrongly) that my body is no part of me, and at other times (correctly) that my body is not an essential part of me.

The other arguments which I have given for the 'simple theory', e.g., that two embodied persons can be the same despite their being no bodily continuity between them, can also, like the argument of Descartes just discussed, if we assume the wider Aristotelian framework, be cast into the form of arguments for classical dualism.

As we have seen, classical dualism is the way of expressing the simple view of personal identity within what I called the wider Aristotelian framework. However, this framework is a wider one than Aristotle himself would have been happy with, allowing a kind of stuff other than Aristotle would have countenanced. There has been in the history of thought a different and very influential way of modifying Aristotle, to take account of the kind of point made by the simple view. This

---

[17] For examples and commentary, see pp. 63–6 of Smart 1977.

way was due to St Thomas Aquinas (see, e.g., *Summa contra Gentiles*). Aquinas accepted Aristotle's general doctrine that substances are made of matter, organized by a form; the desk is the desk which it is because of the matter of which it is made and the shape which is imposed upon it. The form was normally a system of properties, universals which had no existence except in the particular substances in which they were instantiated. However, Aquinas claimed that for man the form of the body, which he called the soul, was separable from the body and capable of independent existence. The soul of man, unlike the souls of animals or plants, was in Aquinas's terminology, an 'intellectual substance'.

However, if we are going to modify Aristotle to make his views compatible with the simple theory of personal identity, this seems definitely the less satisfactory way of doing so. Properties seem by their very nature to be universals and so it is hard to give any sense to their existing except when conjoined to some stuff. Above all, it is hard to give sense to their being individual—a universal can be instantiated in many different substances. What makes the substances differ is the different stuff of which they are composed. The form of man can be instantiated in many different men. But Aquinas wants a form which is a particular, and so could only be combined with one body. All of this seems to involve a greater distortion of Aristotle's system than does classical dualism. Aquinas's system does have some advantages over classical dualism—for example, it enables him to bring out the naturalness of a person being embodied and the temporary and transitory character of any disembodiment—but the disadvantages of taking Aristotle's approach and then distorting it to this unrecognizable extent are in my view very great. Hence my preference for what I have called classical dualism. I shall in future express the simple view in the form of classical dualism, in order to locate this view within the philosophical tradition which seems naturally to express it.

There is, however, one argument often put forward by classical dualists—their argument from the indivisibility of the soul to its natural immortality—from which I must dissociate myself. Before looking at this argument, it is necessary to face the problem of what it means to say that the soul continues to exist. Clearly the soul continues to exist if a person exercises his capacities for experience and action, by having experiences and performing actions. But can the soul continue to exist when the person does not exercise those capacities? Presumably it can. For we say that an unconscious person (who is neither having experiences or acting) is still a person. We say this on the grounds that natural processes (i.e., processes according with the laws of nature) will, or at any rate may, lead to his exercising his capacities again—e.g., through the end of normal sleep or through some medical or surgical intervention. Hence a person, and so his soul, if we talk thus, certainly exists while natural processes may lead to his exercising those capacities again. But what when the person is not exercising his capacities, and no natural processes (whether those operative in our present material universe or those operative in some new world to which the person has moved) will lead to his exercising his capacities? We could say that the person and so his soul still exists on the grounds that there is the logical possibility of his coming to life again. To my mind, the more natural alternative is to say that when ordinary natural processes cannot lead to his exercising his capacities again, a person and so his soul has ceased to exist; but there remains the logical possibility that he may come into existence again (perhaps through God causing him to exist again). One argument against taking the latter alternative is the argument that no substance can have two beginnings of existence. If a person really ceases to exist, then there is not even the logical possibility of his coming into existence again. It would follow that the mere logical possibility of the person coming into existence again has the consequence that a person once existent, is always existent (even when he has no capacity for experience and action). But this principle—that no substance can have two beginnings of existence—is one which I see no good reason for adopting; and if we do not adopt it, then we must say that souls cease to exist when there is no natural possibility of their exercising their capacities. But that does not prevent souls which have ceased to exist coming into existence again. This way of talking does give substantial content to claims that souls do or do not exist, when they are not exercising their capacities.

Now classical dualists assumed (in my view, on balance, correctly) that souls cannot be divided. But they often argued from this, that souls were indestructible,[18] and hence immortal, or at any rate naturally immortal (i.e., immortal as a result of the operation of natural processes, and so immortal barring an act of God to stop those processes operating). That does not follow. Material bodies may lose essential properties without being divided—an oak tree may die and become fossilized without losing its shape. It does not follow from a soul's being indivisible that it cannot lose its capacity for experience and action—and so cease to be a soul. Although there is (I have been arguing) no logical necessity that a soul be linked to a body, it may be physically necessary that a soul be linked to one body if it is to have its essential properties (of capacity for experience and action) and so continue to exist. In section 4 I shall comment briefly on what present evidence shows about whether this is physically necessary.

[18]Thus Berkeley: 'We have shown that the soul is indivisible, incorporeal, unextended, and it is consequently incorruptible' (*Principles*, § 141).

3 Dualism and Verifiability

In this section I shall consider and reject two well-known connected arguments against the dualist view, and then put forward two further substantial arguments in its defence. Much of the discussion turns on claims about the extent of verifiability of claims about personal identity on the dualist view.

My original arguments in favour of the dualist theory were designed to show from brain-transplant considerations that complete knowledge of what has happened to a person's body and its parts, and of the extent of the apparent memory by later persons of the deeds and experiences of the earlier person, would not automatically give knowledge of what has happened to the earlier person, and so that there is more to the continuing of the person than the continuing of his body and apparent memories; subsequent thought-experiments were designed to make the further point that the continuing of the body and apparent memories were inessential for the continuing of the person.

The first counter-argument, which can be found in a succinct form on two pages of Wittgenstein's *Blue Book*, claims that it is a mistake to suppose that there is anything further to be known apart from the fate of the body and its parts and the extent of continuity of apparent memory; there is no further truth about what happens to a person. The supposition that there is arises from the fact that our framework of language and thought was designed for the normal world in which there are no puzzle-cases—no partial brain transplants or men turning up with the same apparent memories as men long-dead, or whatever. Our concepts were designed for the world in which every human body is controlled by one brain which remains intact throughout its operation, no brain parts being added to or subtracted from it, and in which every person with a given body apparently remembers many of the deeds and experiences of the person whose body that body previously was and no deeds and experiences of any other person. In this cosy pre-twenty-first-century world, the questions 'Did he survive?' and 'Is he still alive?' have true and discoverable answers. The survival of the person is guaranteed by the survival of his body and conversely. But it would be wrong to suppose that these questions always have true, let alone discoverable answers, in a world of brain transplants. The only true and relevant statements which can be made in these circumstances will be detailed descriptions of what changes happened to a given body or brain, and what effect some change had on the apparent memories of subsequent persons. There is nothing else informative which can be said; for talk of the survival of the person implies talk of the survival of his whole body, and of much of his apparent memory; and where that does not hold, it would be wrong to say either that he does survive or that he does not. The presuppositions against which such questions can meaningfully be asked are no longer present.

The force of this counter-argument can be brought out by considering a similar issue. Imagine two men arguing fiercely which of the two stars Sirius and Aldebaran is higher up (not higher in the visual field of an observer on Earth, but higher absolutely). One says that Sirius is below Aldebaran, and the other says that Aldebaran is below Sirius. The trouble is that their argument presupposes that there is an absolute up and down, whereas really there is not. 'Below' and 'above' are concepts which only have application on or near a material body, where things fall towards the body and into the body. There one object a is below another b if both are outside the material body but b is further away from it than a; or where b is outside the body but a is on or inside the body; or where both are in or on the body but a is further away from the surface than b. But where objects are in empty space, far from any material body which exercises a gravitational attraction, it is neither true nor false to say that one object is below the other—that Sirius is below Aldebaran, or Aldebaran below Sirius. The situation is the same, says Wittgenstein, with personal identity.

Now it is true that our concepts are devised in certain situations to apply to those situations, and they may well not apply in very different situations. 'Below' and 'above' do not apply in the situation described above; but other concepts devised for certain situations clearly do apply in very different situations. We learn the concept of 'cause' from seeing people cause trees to fall, or animals to die. But having got hold of the concept, we then rightly come to have rival theories about the causes of the recession of the galaxies, or the disintegration of fundamental particles. Or again, interestingly, we learn the concepts of 'being on the left of' and 'being on the right of' (relative to an observer looking from a certain direction) from very mundane situations; but having got the concept, we can then speak of Sirius being to the left of Aldebaran relative to an observer on the Sun. Many concepts derived from certain situations have applications to very different ones. It becomes a Wittgensteinian to show that personal identity is like 'below' and 'above' and not like 'left' and 'right', or 'cause' and 'effect'.

The only argument of which I know put forward at this stage by Wittgensteinians is of a verificationist character, that the only sentences which have a truth value (i.e., are either true or false) are those which can in some sense be verified (i.e., be shown to be true or false). They then claim that as you cannot verify whether a man survives a brain-transplant operation, the claim that he does is neither true nor false.

Now verificationism is a big philosophical issue, and a full discussion is impossible in an essay devoted to another issue, but I do need to make some brief remarks on the nature and justification of verificationism and its relevance to our issue. The general feeling which leads to verificationism is the feeling that we can only understand a sentence if we know what in experience will correspond to its truth. But, although that feeling may be a correct one, we can justify it in terms of a doctrine which I have called elsewhere[19] 'word-verificationism' and which is very different from verificationism proper. Word-verificationism is the doctrine that we can understand a sentence, i.e., that it has a meaning in our language, if and only if the words which occur in it have a meaning and the sentence is grammatically well formed; the words have a meaning if and only if they are empirically cashable; and the sentence is grammatically well formed if and only if the grammatical pattern in which the words are put together is empirically cashable. If the sentence which has a meaning is declarative (i.e., grammatically indicative), then it will have a truth value

---

[19]See Swinburne 1983. The main part of this paper (pp. 63–70) is a discussion of verificationism with particular reference to the 'anti-realism' of Michael Dummett. Some points from this paper are repeated here.

(i.e., be true or false). By the words being 'empirically cashable' I mean that they occur in other sentences which are verifiable or falsifiable, and that they make there a difference to their verification conditions. Thus the word 'metre' is empirically cashable because it occurs in sentences like 'this table is two metres long' which can be verified or falsified by measuring the table, and it makes a difference to the verification conditions (e.g., if we leave it out we have an unverifiable sentence, and if we replace it by 'inches' we have a sentence which is verified or falsified by different experimental results). By the grammatical pattern of the sentence being empirically cashable, I mean that the words are joined together (e.g., a predicate is attributed to a subject term, or it is said that all objects characterized by a certain predicate are also characterized by a certain other one) in ways in which they are joined together in other sentences which are verifiable or falsifiable.[20] Word verificationism is a

---

[20]This demand that the sentence be grammatically well-formed may be understood in a wider or a narrower way. In the wider way, the demand is simply a demand that the sentence have the same syntactical structure as some verifiable sentence. Thus if a given verb only makes a verifiable sentence when followed by an object-term, then it must be followed by an object-term in any sentence which is to be grammatically well formed. Thus 'John opens' is not grammatically well formed, because 'opens' is always followed by an object-term in verifiable sentences. We need to say 'John opens the door' or 'John opens a book', to have a sentence with truth value. This kind of grammatical formation is the kind with which grammarians deal. Yet it allows such sentences as 'Saturday opens the door' or 'truth has four equal sides' to have truth value. Many philosophers have wished to deny truth value to such sentences claiming that they are 'meaningless' because they commit some sort of category mistake. To form a sentence with a truth value it is no good inserting any referring expression into the gap in ' . . . opens the door'. You have to insert a referring expression which picks out a substance, maybe even necessarily a living substance, not a period of time. So 'John opens the door' or 'the dog opens the door' have truth value, whereas 'Saturday opens the door' does not. To insist that similarity of form to that of verifiable sentences include similarity in respect not merely of syntax but of categories, yields a more restrictive form of word-verificationism. To spell it out, we would need a satisfactory philosophical doctrine of categories—i.e., a doctrine of the kinds of thing which can exist, and the kinds of property which things of different kinds can possess. ('Can' here is the logical 'can'. Our concern would be with a logical possibility of different kinds of thing possessing properties of different kinds.) Yet the restriction seems to me an unnecessary one. It seems not unnatural to say that 'Saturday opens the door' is not meaningless, like a collection of mumbo-jumbo expressions or even like 'John opens', but comprehensible and false. However, in either form word-verificationism is a doctrine which makes whether a sentence has a truth value depend, not on its own verifiability, but on the verifiability of similar sentences.

The narrower version of word-verificationism would rule out, as not having a truth value, the sentences discussed in the text 'Aldebaran is below Sirius' and 'Sirius is below Aldebaran' on the ground that Aldebaran and Sirius are not objects of the right category to be above or below each other. The wider version of word-verificationism would hold

highly plausible doctrine, the first part of which concerning the need for words to be empirically cashable was affirmed in effect by philosophers as diverse as Aquinas and Hume,[21] both of whom would probably have been happy to assent to the second part also.

But verificationism proper goes beyond word-verificationism in insisting that if it is to have a truth value, a sentence has itself to be verifiable or falsifiable. The sentence 'there is in the universe somewhere an uninhabited planet on which yesterday (by the cosmic time scale) there was an explosion' can according to this doctrine only be true or false if there is some way of verifying or falsifying it. Verificationism proper has a multitude of different forms, according to the strength of the verification on which we insist, by whom and when the verification has to be performable (by some person, or by any person; now or at some time or other), and whether the possibility of verification has to be a logical possibility, a physical possibility or a practical possibility. Are we to insist on the possibility of infallible verification (or falsification), i.e., verification (or falsification) of such a kind that we cannot possibly be mistaken, verification 'beyond reasonable doubt'; or simply confirmation or disconfirmation, i.e., the possibility of having some evidence which supports or counts against the truth of the sentence?

For myself I cannot see adequate justification for adopting any of these forms of verificationism proper. So long as we understand the grammatical pattern of a declarative sentence and the words which occur in it we understand what claims it is making,

---

both these sentences to have the truth value false just because Aldebaran and Sirius are not objects in or near an attracting material body. In discussing this example I took for granted the account which would be given by the narrower version, since this is more congenial to the Wittgensteinian approach; but my point could have been made in a way conforming to the wider version.

For further exposition of word-verificationism see Swinburne 1983, and also Sklar 1980 which is basically sympathetic to the doctrine (to which it gives a different name) but which exhibits the difficulties of spelling it out, such as those described above.

[21]Thus Hume held that words which purport to denote 'ideas', i.e., in modern terms properties, do so only if we have had 'impressions' of them, i.e., observed instances of them. See Hume, *Treatise*, p. 22. Aquinas quotes Aristotle with approval for holding that 'our knowledge begins from the senses' (*Summa Theologiae*, Ia 84. 6), and he held that the meanings of predicates applied to God 'are known to us solely to the extent that they are said of creatures'. It has been the recent programme of Donald Davidson to show how the meanings of compound sentences derive from their constituents. See, for example, Davidson 1969.

even if we have no conceivable means of getting evidence for its truth or falsity. To suppose otherwise, to suppose that anything which man can understand he can to some extent verify or falsify, seems to attribute to man a certain kind of omniscience. However, verificationism proper only becomes remotely plausible if we take a fairly weak version of it. If we insist on the possibility of infallible verification or falsification, it is doubtful if very many sentences, or indeed any at all, would have a truth value. It is doubtful whether we can verify or falsify infallibly even such a sentence as 'there is a table in this room'. Whatever our sense experiences, we might be subject to illusion, or we might be dreaming. But then of how strong a verification or falsification does a sentence need to be susceptible in order to have a truth value? There is clearly a continuous quantitative gradation between 'beyond reasonable doubt' and mere confirmation. We can have some evidence for a sentence, or a bit more, or a bit more still, and if we have enough that puts the sentence 'beyond reasonable doubt' (though what counts as 'reasonable doubt' about the truth of some sentence is not a function solely of the amount of evidence in its favour but of the importance to the investigator in the circumstances of his life in being right about it). Some sentences are susceptible of stronger verification and falsification than others. One can get stronger evidence in favour of 'there are no unicorns on Earth' than in favour of 'there are no unicorns anywhere in our galaxy', and stronger evidence in favour of the latter than in favour of 'there are no unicorns anywhere in the universe'. But any attempt to say that a sentence has a truth value only if it is capable of verification or falsification to such-and-such a degree, would seem highly arbitrary. How are degrees of verifiability to be measured, or how are we to choose that degree which is necessary? The natural thing to say is that any degree of verifiability or falsifiability is enough. A sentence has a truth value so long as it is confirmable or disconfirmable, i.e., some evidence can be had for or against it. Examples support this suggestion. We naturally allow that all three sentences about unicorns have a truth value, even if we can be less sure what that truth value is in some cases than in others.

But then so long as we insist only on the possibility of confirmation or disconfirmation, whether we demand that the possibility be logical, physical or practical, the confirmation be done by one person or anybody, now or at some time or other, the dualist theory of personal identity will not fall foul of verificationism. For the claim that person P_2, recovering from a brain operation, is the same person as a person P_1 before the operation can certainly have evidence in its favour—e.g., that P_2 has some of P_1's brain and most of his apparent memories (as publicly evidenced, by his public memory claims). If some other present person P_2^* also turns out to have some of P_1's brain and some of his apparent memories, this counts against P_2 being the same as P_1—P_2^* not being the same person as P_2, evidence favouring P_2^* being the same person as P_1 counts against P_2 being the same person as P_1.

The amount of brain and memory continuity may favour one or other of P_2 and P_2^* being P_1. It is possible that on current evidence P_2 and P_2^* may be equally good candidates for being P_1. But even if this is so, there always remains the possibility of further evidence turning up favouring one against the other—e.g., although today P_2 and P_2^* have apparent memories which correspond equally well with incidents in P_1's life, tomorrow P_2 may continue to produce apparent memories which correspond well whereas P_2^*'s apparent memories cease to correspond well. Or, it may turn out later that although it originally appeared that P_2 and P_2^* had an equal amount of P_1's brain matter, in fact most of P_1's brain matter went to P_2. We are never in the position where it is not logically possible that any further evidence turn up concerning which of P_2 and P_2^* is P_1.

The possibility of verifying claims about personal identity is a practical one, can be performed at any time (though obviously more efficiently immediately after any transplant), and can be performed by any person (though obviously a subject is the best source of knowledge about his own apparent memories). Verificationism is a dubious doctrine, but even if we allow it, any of its more plausible forms are quite inadequate to defeat my claim that there is a truth whether a later person is the same person as a certain earlier person, which is not entailed by information about what happens to the earlier person's brain and the extent of continuity of apparent memory between them —although this information may provide non-conclusive evidence about whether the two persons are the same.

I conclude that the Wittgensteinian 'counter-argument' fails because there is no real argument there. It is simply a dogmatic assertion that the concept of personal identity has no application in puzzle situations, which is not backed up by any adequate argument.

Part of the apparent force of the counter-argument derived, I believe, from the implicit suggestion that claims about personal identity were always matters of inference, never matters of experience—in the sense that although it might sometimes be obvious that some later person was the same as a certain earlier person, nevertheless any claim about personal identity received its ultimate justification in terms of something closer to experience, viz., bodily or brain continuity, and similarity of apparent memory. Any claim about personal identity, if disputed, could be settled, if at all, only by studying these latter phenomena, more evident to experience.

In general, of course, my own argument has been that personal identity is something evidenced but not constituted by, bodily continuity and memory similarity. I now however wish to make the point that the continuing existence of a person over a very short period of time is something which can often be experienced by that person. It is something of which we are often aware without our knowledge of it depending on our knowledge of anything more ultimate. In that sense the continuing of a person is a datum of experience; and if it were not, we could have little knowledge of the world.

Human experience is experience of change. The perceptual beliefs to which our senses give rise are not just beliefs that at one time things were arranged thus, and at another time in a different way, and at a third time in yet a third way. For as a result of experience we come to know not merely what happened but in what order things happened—that first things were arranged like this, and subsequently like that, and yet subsequently like that. Sometimes of course we infer from our experiences and our general knowledge of how things happen in the world, the order in which those experiences must have occurred. Knowing that in general babies get bigger and not smaller I may infer that my seeing the small baby John occurred before my seeing the medium sized baby John, which occurred before my seeing the large baby John. But not all knowledge of the order of our experiences can derive from inference. For first we have much knowledge of the actual order of experiences, when as far as our general knowledge of the world goes, the events experienced could as easily occur in one order as in the other. As far as my general knowledge of the world goes, birds in the sky are as likely to fly from left to right in a man's field of vision as from right to left. My knowledge that on a particular occasion my experience of seeing a bird on my left preceded my experience of seeing it on my right could not be an inference from the normal behaviour of birds. And secondly, that general knowledge of the normal temporal order in which events occur must itself derive from experience if it is to be justified and so amount to knowledge. Knowledge that events of type A normally precede events of type B must be grounded in many observations made by ourselves or others of actual such successions.

So our knowledge of change arising from sense-experience must include experience of change which is not grounded in a more basic experience of something else. We observe things happening in a certain order. The most primitive things which an observer sees include not just the train being here, but also the train moving from here to there, from there to the third place. When a train moves along a railway line, the observer S on the bank has the following successive experiences: S sees train T at place p followed by T at place q; S sees T at q followed by T at r; S sees T at r followed by T at u, and so on. But then that is not quite a full description of his experience. For if those were all the data of experience, S would need to infer that the second experience which I have described succeeded the first (rather than being one which occurred on an entirely different occasion). Why he does not need to infer this is because it is itself also a datum of experience; S experiences his experiences as overlapping as in a stream of awareness. As John Foster, to whom I owe the above argument puts it, 'it is this double overlap which provides the sensible continuity of sense experience and unifies presentations' (i.e., perceptual experiences) 'into a stream of awareness' (Foster 1979, p. 176). And what the subject of experience is aware of is of those experiences as his, that is as having a common subject. For the subject in claiming that not merely his present experience of the world but the experiences which stream into it are his, is claiming that one person experiences them. As Foster puts it, 'it is in the unity of a stream that we primarily discern the identity of a subject'. So my experience of continuing change is the experience that my experiences of certain small changes are experienced in succession by a common subject.

Hume wrote: 'When I enter most intimately into what I call *myself*, I always stumble on some particular perception or other, of heat or cold, light or shade, love or hatred, pain or pleasure. I never catch *myself* at any time without a perception' (*Treatise* Bk I Pt IV § VI). It may well be that Hume never catches himself without a perception but his bare data are not just perceptions, but successions of overlapping perceptions experienced by a common subject. If it were not so, we would have no grounded knowledge of succession. Hume says that he fails to find the 'self', i.e., the common subject. One wonders what he supposed that the common subject would look like, and what he considered would count as its discovery. Was he looking for a common element in all his visual fields, or a background noise which never ceased? Is that the sort of thing he failed to find?[22] Yet the self which he ought to have found in all his experiences is supposed to be the subject, not the object of experience. And finding it consists in being aware of different experiences as had by the same subject. These may be successive experiences, as have been my concern so far; and, as we have seen, without such awareness our claims about the order of events in the world would be groundless; and if that was so, so would be all claims about the fate of the brain, and indeed all claims about the operation of the natural world.

A person exists, I suggested in section 2, only in so far as he has the capacity for having experiences and performing actions. He need not be exercising those capacities, but it must be naturally possible (in the sense delineated in section 2) and so at any rate logically possible that he do so. It follows that it must be logically possible that a person have experiences of his

---

[22]Because our awareness of ourselves is different in kind from our awareness of objects of experience, Berkeley chose to say that we have a 'notion' of the former but an 'idea' of the latter. 'To expect that by any multiplication or enlargement of our faculties we may be enabled to know a spirit as we do a triangle, seems as absurd as if we should hope to see a sound' (Berkeley, *Principles*, § 142).

continuing existence at each moment of that existence. Now no person could have the experience of himself as being formed from the fusion of two persons (in the way described on p. 21 above). For suppose P_2 to be formed from the fusion of P_1 and P_1^*. If P_2 was so formed and having experiences while being so formed, it would seem that he must have two incompatible experiences at the same time. He would have to experience himself as experiencing P_1's experiences in a continuing stream as they occur and coming suddenly to acquire awareness of P_1^*'s experiences subsequent to their occurrence; and also as experiencing P_1^*'s experiences in a continuing stream as they occur and coming suddenly to acquire awareness of P_1's experiences subsequent to their occurrence. The experience of fusion cannot be described coherently; which suggests that the subsequent person cannot in any real sense to any degree be both persons, for if he could, he ought to be able to some extent to have experienced both their experiences. But that would not be logically possible, for he could not in any way simultaneously be aware of P_1's experiences while coming to know P_1^*'s, and be aware of P_1^*'s experiences while coming to know P_1's. This argument against the logical possibility of fusion backs up the previous argument (of p. 18) against the logical possibility of fission, and so completes my defence of the thesis of the indivisibility of the soul (see p. 21 above), which claims that neither fission nor fusion is logically possible. However, the indivisibility thesis is not my central thesis, and my arguments in its favour have in consequence been brief ones.

My first further argument in favour of my main thesis, the dualist theory, was that the continuing existence of a person over time is often something experienced by that person. My second further argument claims that among the data of experience are not merely that certain experiences are the successive experiences of a common subject, but also that certain simultaneous experiences are the experiences of a common subject. At a single moment of time you feel cramp in your leg, hear the noise of my voice, and see the movement of my arms. It is among the data of your experience, something of which you are often aware without your knowledge of it depending on anything more ultimate, that these are all your experiences.

Yet that experiences are experiences of the same subject is

something that knowledge of brains and their states and knowledge of which experiences were occurring would be insufficient to tell you. A brain operation sometimes performed is cerebral commissurotomy—cutting the tract between the two hemispheres. As I noted earlier, in the normal brain some signals (including those from the right ear and right sides of the two eyes) go in the first instance to the left hemisphere and some (including those from the left ear and left sides of the two eyes) to the right hemisphere; and the hemispheres control different parts of the body (the left hemisphere controlling speech, as well as the right arm and leg). However, in the normal brain the signals to one hemisphere are immediately transmitted to the other, and the instructions given by one are correlated with events in the other. But if a cerebral commissurotomy is performed, the hemispheres act in a much more independent way, and it is a crucial issue whether by the operation we have created two persons. Experimenters seek to discover by the responses in speech, writing or other means, whether one subject is co-experiencing all the different visual, auditory, olfactory, etc., stimuli, or whether there are two subjects each of whom have different experiences. Mere knowledge that the two hemispheres are connected much less directly than previously, will not tell you whether you have one or two subjects of experience.

The only way for investigators to find out is to try to get reports from the subject (or subjects) about what they are experiencing. If they elicit from organs of the body in question two simultaneous reports reporting different packages of sensations, that will suggest that there are two persons; whereas if at any one time they get only reports of the same package of sensations, that will suggest that there is only one person. However, further factors also have to be taken into account. If the mouth confesses to seeing a green object but not to hearing a loud noise; while the left hand denies seeing a green object, but claims instead to hear a loud noise, that is not enough in itself to show that no subject both experienced a loud noise and saw a green object. For, first, mouth and hand may sometimes, as may any limb, give a reflex response to a question rather than a considered judgement (the reflex may be out of a subject's control without being in the control of some other subject); and secondly, there may be kinds of information which the subject can only convey by one means rather than another. The effect of cerebral commissurotomy is not immediately evident, and various complex experiments are needed before any one hypothesis about what has happened can gain significant support.[23] But what is clear is that what the investigator is trying to discover is something other than and beyond the pattern of the subject's responses, as it is also something other than and beyond the extent of the connections between the two hemispheres. That something is naturally described as whether there are one or two subjects of experience.

It might be said that the issue is much simpler, and the alternatives can be stated without bringing in the concept of a person, a subject of experience. What the investigator is trying to discover, it may be said, is whether there is one total experience, consisting of various visual, auditory, etc., elements; or whether there are two simultaneous experiences—one consisting of a visual sensation, say, and the other of cramp in the left leg. But what does it mean to say that there are two distinct but simultaneous experiences? Why should I not say of my own experiences at this moment, that there are a number of distinct experiences going on simultaneously? In a sense that is so; there are. There is an experience of a blue flash and also an experience of cramp in the left leg. But in a crucial sense there are not distinct experiences. And what is that crucial sense? That there is one total experience of a blue flash and of cramp in the left leg? But it would be unnatural to say that anyone had an experience of-a-blue-flash-and-cramp-in-the-left-leg, unless, as it were, he felt them to be connected—as he might if they were both produced through his touching some piece of electrical apparatus. Yet they might be felt to have no connection with each other, and so there not be in a natural sense any one experience of a blue flash and cramp in the left leg. No, the only way to bring out the sense in question in which the experiences are not distinct is to say that they are experiences of a common subject. One person is having both experiences. And he is often aware of doing so. In simultaneous experience, as in experience over time, the unity of experience is something of which the subject is often aware and no mere inference from the unity of

[23]On the results and interpretation of such experiments, see Mackay and Mackay 1982.

brain or behaviour. Here too, the existence of persons as subjects of experiences is an unanalysable fact of which we are sometimes aware and not one which we are justified in affirming on the basis of other data closer to experience. That there are at an instant persons, as well as bodies, brains, and experiences makes it natural to suppose that the continuing of persons over time is also a fact other than and beyond data about the continuing of bodies, brains and experiences over time—as has been the main argument of this essay so far.

4 The Evidence of Personal Identity

I have argued that although personal identity is unanalysable in terms of continuity of brain and apparent memory, it is usefully defined as consisting in the continuing existence of a soul, while continuity of brain and apparent memory (backed up by continuity of character) provide fallible evidence of personal identity. I need now to give an explanation of how it is, on the dualist view, that continuity of brain and apparent memory are evidence of personal identity. For on other views of the nature of personal identity it is easy to give an account of why continuity of brain and memory should be evidence of it. If personal identity simply consists in continuity of memory, then of course continuity of memory shows personal identity. It is found empirically that if P_1 has brain B and P_2 also has brain B (or perhaps only part of it), then in most cases there is continuity of memory between P_1 and P_2, and conversely; and hence on a particular occasion brain continuity is evidence of personal identity. Alternatively if personal identity simply consists in continuity of brain, as that part of the body which is normally causally responsible for memory and character, of course continuity of memory is evidence of personal identity. But if personal identity can exist without either continuity of brain or apparent memory, how is it that they are evidence of it?

Before answering this crucial question, it is important to give an account of the fact that normally we make judgements of personal identity (e.g., 'this is the man whom I saw last week') by using tests quite other than bodily or brain continuity or continuity of memory. The most frequent test to be used is the test of similarity of visual appearance. We judge this man to be the man whom I saw last week because he looks like him. To similarity of visual appearance, we must add similarity of appearance to the other senses—e.g., sound of voice (and, no doubt, for people with poor vision and hearing, smell or feel). Similarity of a person's appearance covers not only instantaneous appearance, but appearance over time in the ways in which he manifests his presence—e.g., the way he walks and the gestures he makes. More technical tests used today are sameness of fingerprints and blood groups.

Evidently the latter tests are used because they are evidence that other of the tests, more difficult to apply, would be satisfied if we could use them. We use fingerprints as evidence of personal identity because of a discovery in the nineteenth century that when two persons are by other criteria pretty conclusively the same, they have the same fingerprints, and when two persons are by other criteria pretty conclusively distinct, they have distinct fingerprints. That suggests that when we have evidence of sameness of fingerprints but not evidence one way or the other about (e.g.) bodily continuity, nevertheless bodily continuity holds. Fingerprints are thus indirect evidence of personal identity, in the sense that they are evidence of what would be shown by other and so more central criteria of personal identity. The same evidently goes for blood groups and other physiological tests.

What of similarity of appearance? It too, I would suggest is an indirect test in the stated sense. We take similarity of appearance at different times as evidence of personal identity because we believe it to be evidence of bodily identity and this (via brain identity) to be evidence of personal identity. We do this because we believe that in general each body has a distinctive appearance—two bodies observed at different times which are to all appearances qualitatively indistinguishable are very probably the same body; and two bodies observed at different times which are qualitatively distinct in appearance are very probably different bodies. This principle is modified in various ways which we have by experience found necessary. First appearance changes gradually with time; faces become lined, hair becomes grey. We know this because we observe that often a body which we judge to be the same as a body observed on the previous day on the basis of its similarity of appearance, and to be the same as a body on the day before that, on the basis of the similarity of that to the body on the middle day, and so on until you reach a body years earlier, looks different if you compare its appearance directly with its appearance years earlier. Having discovered empirically the ways in which appearances change, we can then allow for these (i.e., discount difference in appearance of bodies observed at intervals of a number of years in respect of face lining and hair colour) in judging similarity of appearance.

Also, we learn empirically (from those who have kept bodies under continuous observation and judged them to be the same body on the basis of similarity of appearance of most of their parts) that sometimes some parts of bodies (e.g., faces as a result of plastic surgery) change their appearance very quickly. But because such events are rare, we take radical difference of appearance to show distinctness of body, in the absence of evidence of the occurrence of such an event as plastic surgery. Also we learn empirically, by seeing them side by side, that sometimes two different bodies are indistinguishable in appearance. (There are identical twins.) And in those cases we hesitate to take similarity of appearance as evidence of sameness of body.

But, although in this way similarity of appearance is, like fingerprints, an indirect criterion of bodily identity, it seems to me that we did not discover that bodies have in general a constant and distinctive appearance over periods of time by keeping a random sample of bodies under continuous observation and finding that they change their appearance only rarely, and that identical twins are rare. For, after all, any observer who tries to keep a body B under continuous observation would need sometimes to go to sleep. So in order to check that B does not change appearance by night, he must hand over to a different observer O. Yet the reports of an observer P in the morning that the body which he observed did not change its appearance overnight are only of use if P is the same observer as O, and the grounds for supposing that he is are not observed bodily continuity, but rather observed similarity of appearance.

The position is rather that, when we do keep bodies under observation for a limited period, any great change of appearance is very rare indeed, and bodies of totally similar appearance are also very rare indeed. It is simpler to suppose that this constancy and distinctness of appearance holds when bodies are not under observation, as well as when they are; rather than to suppose that things change suddenly when we are not observing them.

So then similarity of appearance at different times is an indirect criterion of personal identity, because it is evidence of bodily identity which in turn is evidence of personal identity. But we have already seen in section 1 that bodily identity is only used as evidence as personal identity, given that the body retains the same brain. In other words, because brain transplants (very probably) do not yet occur, bodily identity is now well-nigh conclusive evidence of brain identity. So it too is indirect evidence of personal identity. And why is brain identity so important? We choose the brain as the organ whose continuity is vital for personal identity because it is that organ, the continuity of which guarantees continuity of apparent memory and character. Given that P_2 and an earlier P_1 have the same brains, P_2 will in general apparently remember the deeds and experiences of P_1 and behave in somewhat similar ways to P_1. And given (as neurophysiology leads us reasonably to suppose) that if brains are split, both hemispheres or smaller parts of the brain would bring about some continuity of apparent memory and character in the persons into whose skulls they were transplanted, it is brain continuity (i.e., material continuity of whatever parts of the brain are causally responsible for apparent memory and character), which is evidence of personal identity. Our selection of brain continuity as evidence of personal identity because that is the part of the body which is correlated with continuity of apparent memory and character, suggests that but for a correlation with apparent memory and character we would not use any part of the body as evidence of personal identity.

We can see that that is so by asking ourselves what we would say if the following occurred. Suppose that a person in body B_1 on even days apparently remembered (almost) everything done and experienced by the person in that body on even days, and (almost) everything done and experienced by the person in another body B_2 on odd days, but nothing done and experienced by the person in B_1 on odd days nor anything done and experienced by the person in B_2 on even days. The person in B_2 on odd days has the same apparent memories as the person in B_1 on even days. Conversely the person in B_1 on odd days and the person in B_2 on even days have the same apparent memories, which concern the deeds and experiences only of the person in B_1 on odd days and the person in B_2 on even days. Suppose too that character goes with apparent memory (e.g., that the persons in B_1 on odd days and B_2 on even days have the same character), and that there are no transplants of any parts of the body.

If this kind of apparent body-swap was a normal, regular, exceptionless feature of life, it seems patently obvious that we would not claim that bodily continuity (or continuity of any part of the body) ensured personal identity. What might be more open to question is whether we would then claim that a person was who he apparently remembered that he was. Might we not suppose instead that persons lasted for only one day? It seems to me unlikely that we would suppose this in view of the enormous continuity of memory, general beliefs and attitudes towards the world which I suppose to hold between people in different bodies on different days. I suggest that in these circumstances not merely would we suppose that personal identity went with apparent memory, but that we would be right to suppose this. To justify this claim, I shall now give a general argument for the primacy of the criterion of apparent memory, ignoring for the moment the role of continuity of character. (I shall come back to that later.)

Recall that by apparent memory we mean apparent personal memory, and this is simply what it seems to a man that he did or experienced in the past, not on the basis of anything else (e.g., what it seems to him that he has been told, or read in a diary), but seems straight off. We noted in section 1 that apparent memories may be shown in various ways not to be genuine memories—e.g., by it being shown that what was apparently remembered did not happen to anyone, or that the cause of the subject's apparent memory was his being told what happened by someone else, which acted on him so as to give him a new belief and not to revivify an old one. But although apparent memories may be shown not to be genuine memories, they are, I suggest, to be taken at their face value as evidence of that of which they are apparent memories, in the absence of counter-evidence. This follows the most basic principle for making inferences from experience to the world, which I have called elsewhere the principle of credulity.[24] That states that probably things are as (in the epistemic sense[25]) they seem to be—e.g., if

---

[24]The arguments which I give here in support of this principle are very brief. For much fuller argument, see Swinburne 1979, pp. 254–71.

[25]As Chisholm pointed out (1957, ch. 4), there are at least two uses of 'seems', 'appears' (and similar verbs for specific senses: 'looks', 'sounds', 'feels', etc.). To say that something looks (in the comparative sense) to a man elliptical is to say that it looks the

it seems to me that there is in front of me a brown table, or a Greek vase, then probably there is; and I ought so to believe, unless counter-evidence turns up. My apparent memory that I did or experienced so-and-so is just it seeming to me that I did or experienced so-and-so; that I am justified in believing my apparent memories in the absence of counter-evidence follows from the principle of credulity. Relying on it involves applying the principle to a special kind of case (how things seem with regard to my past deeds and experiences). Any attempt to deny the principle of credulity and say that you are not justified in believing things, solely because they seem so, and that you need further evidence, will lead to a very deep scepticism. Thus suppose that a philosopher says that you should not believe that there is in front of you a brown table, just because it seems to you there is; and that you need some further evidence that when it seems to you that there is a brown table in front of you there really is. Such evidence might be that when in the past it has seemed to you that there is a brown table in front of you, subsequent experience has borne this out, e.g., if you apparently put your hands in front of you you have feelings of a table, and you have subsequent brown visual experiences. But if you need that kind of evidence before you are justified in believing that when it seems to you that there is a brown table in front of you there really is, then the question arises as to how you are to know that you have had these past experiences, and the answer is going to be because it seems to you to have been thus, i.e., that you apparently so remember. The dependence on apparent memory is a special unavoidable case of application of the principle of credulity. And if the principle of credulity suffices to justify reliance on apparent memories, it suffices also to justify reliance on apparent perceptions, such as there being a brown table in front of you, without appeal to anything further, such as apparent memories.

An objector might say that one is justified in believing one's

something looks (in the comparative sense) to a man elliptical is to say that it looks the way elliptical things normally look. The man to whom something looks elliptical, or red, or a long way away, may be in no way deceived by appearances. Whereas to say that something looks (in the epistemic sense, or epistemically) elliptical to a man is to say that he is inclined to believe (on the basis of the way it looks) that it is elliptical; to say that something seems, appears, looks, elliptical, red, or a long way away is to report what appearances suggest about how things are.

apparent memory only if it coincides with the apparent memory of someone else. But a man often believes his memory of what he alone has seen, and intuitively it seems right so to do. Anyway, after someone else has born testimony to his apparent memory which coincides with yours, your subsequent reliance on the joint memory depends on your own apparent memory of the coincidence between what you did and what he claimed to remember.

Any belief which we reach through application of the principle of credulity is corrigible. Suppose a certain metal object viewed from a certain angle looks (in the epistemic sense) elliptical. I therefore come to believe that it is elliptical. But when I view it from several other angles it looks (in the epistemic sense) round and when I feel it it feels round. So I come to believe that when I perceive it on the latter occasions it is round. It is simpler to suppose that it has always remained of the same shape rather than that it has suddenly changed shape (which would make it unlike other metal objects, which, use of the principle of credulity leads us to suppose, do not change shape suddenly). So I come to believe that it has always been round, and retract my original judgement that on a certain occasion it was elliptical. But my retraction depends crucially on my use of the principle of credulity on other occasions, and on the results produced by many users of it outweighing the result produced by a single use. There is no other access to justified beliefs about the world except by means of the principle of credulity. If you refuse to believe anything until you have other evidence for it, you will never believe anything —for as we saw earlier you can only have access to a body of past evidence by means of the principle of credulity. But if you start by believing everything which you are inclined to believe until you have evidence against it, you will have a normal belief system. And given, as I assume, that such a system is a well-justified system, it follows that reliance as the principle of credulity is justified.

All access to the past, I would claim, depends ultimately on apparent personal memory. But even if I am wrong about this it certainly depends on some form of knowledge which is ultimately authenticated by the principle of credulity. Plausibly, I can only use my diary to learn about the past if I apparently remember that I wrote it; and I can only use geological methods if someone apparently remembers that the theory which has the consequence that they are reliable gave many successful predictions, and I apparently remember being so told by him. Even if I am wrong to suppose that all access to the past depends on apparent personal memory, it clearly depends in the first instance on apparent factual memory. In talking so far about apparent memory, I have, as I stated, been talking about apparent personal memory. My personal memory is my memory of what I personally did and experienced; this is to be contrasted with factual memory which is memory of certain facts—e.g., that $5 \times 7 = 35$ or that the Battle of Hastings was fought in 1066. Now it is true that we often rely for our knowledge of the world on apparent factual memory. I claim to know now that the Battle of Hastings was fought in 1066 on the basis of memory, and I mean by this that I previously knew it to be the case. Factual memory is present knowledge caused by past knowledge; I know now because I knew then and have not forgotten. Apparent factual memory is apparent knowledge apparently caused by past knowledge. It follows from the principle of credulity that I am justified in believing apparent factual memory to be indeed knowledge caused by past knowledge.

Now I am inclined to think that it would not seem to me that I had previously known that the Battle of Hastings was fought in 1066, unless it also seemed to me that on some occasion or other (which I may not now be able to recall) I had discovered by historical inquiry or been told by others that the Battle of Hastings was fought in 1066; that is unless it could be backed up by apparent personal memory (at least, of this very indefinite kind). So I am inclined to hold that all knowledge of the past depends ultimately on apparent personal memory. I may, however, be wrong about this. Maybe there can be apparent factual memories which are not backed up in this way;[26] or maybe apparent factual memories can be backed up by apparent 'quasi-memories' or 'Q-memories', of the kind described by Shoemaker (1970a) and subsequently by Parfit (1971b). Q-memory is memory 'from the inside' of what was done and experienced without the rememberer in any way seeming to remember that it was he himself who had experienced

[26]As Wittgenstein seems to claim in *On Certainty*.

it. A Q-memory is an ordinary personal memory minus the belief that the subject himself did the deeds or had the experiences. A man might remember having been to London with all the detail of what it felt like, looked like, and how the doer made decisions to go to one museum and then to another, without it in any way seeming to the rememberer that it was he himself who had gone to London. I do not think that anybody these days has Q-memories; but it seems that there could be memory of that kind, and maybe the development of brain transplants could lead to people having Q-memories. In that case we might regard it as sufficient justification for an apparent factual memory that it was backed up by an apparent Q-memory. But then our reliance on apparent Q-memory ('it seems to me that someone went to London') could receive its justification only from the principle of credulity itself.

So the principle of credulity is essential for the justification of our claims to knowledge of the past, and it suffices to justify our reliance on apparent personal memory. All its deliverances are to be relied on in the absence of counter-evidence. So our reliance on apparent personal memory, as a criterion for telling us which past person a person was, is justified a priori,[27] and it can show which other criteria are reliable. This general argument confirms that in the apparent body-swap thought-experiment, we would be right to judge that a person was who he apparently remembered that he was.

The principle of credulity also justifies our reliance on what I called in Section 3 our 'experience' of our own personal identity over the very short period, and which, to conform to the terminology of this section, I can now call our 'apparent experience' (e.g., it seeming to me now epistemically that I am the common subject of such-and-such successive or simultaneous experiences). I called this 'seeming' an 'experience' in Section 3 to make the point that it was not and could not be an inference from anything else, but I now call it an 'apparent experience' to make the point that, though to be relied upon, it

[27]Butler gives an argument of this kind for relying on apparent memory as evidence of personal identity, concluding that 'it is ridiculous to attempt to prove the truth of those perceptions, whose truth we can not otherwise prove, than by other perceptions of exactly the same kind with them, and which there is just the same ground to suspect; or to attempt to prove the truth of our faculties, which can not otherwise be proved, by the use of means of those very suspected faculties themselves'.

is fallible. The line of division between apparent experience and apparent memory is a somewhat arbitrary one.

So brain continuity provides only indirect evidence of personal identity; our justification for using it is that in general when and only when two persons P_2 at t_2 and P_1 at t_1 are connected by continuity of apparent memory[28] (viz., P_2 apparently remembers the deeds and experiences of P_1 or is connected by a chain of such persons in the way outlined in section 1) they also have the same brain; and that is reason to suppose that where parts of brains are transplanted, persons connected at any rate by some continuity of brain matter are also connected by continuity of apparent memory. This evidence of what almost invariably happens makes brain continuity in some particular case strong evidence of personal identity—in the absence of counter-evidence—when we do not have any evidence from apparent memory.

But what about where a person P_2 has no apparent memory of the deeds and experiences of P_1, even though he tries to recall such deeds and experiences; and what about where the two criteria are in conflict? Suppose that P_2 at t_2 has the same brain as P_1 but apparent memory of the deeds and experiences of some person P_1^* at t_1, with whom no other person at t_2 has continuity of brain or apparent memory? Shall we say that P_2 is P_1 or that he is P_1^*?

Here a different factor enters in. One would expect apparent memory to be sometimes in error. Just as I sometimes misobserve things in front of me now and misremember facts about the positions and properties of material bodies, so one would expect me sometimes to misremember what I did and experienced. That people sometimes misremember their deeds and experiences is shown by the fact that it can sometimes be shown that no one did what they claim to have done. It is also shown by the fact that application of the criterion of apparent memory can sometimes yield results in conflict with itself. A senile P_2 may apparently remember both the deeds of P_1 at t_1 and the deeds of P_1^* at t_1, and yet since P_1 and P_1^* had no awareness of each other's deeds at the time in question they are clearly different persons.

[28]Henceforward, again, I shall understand by 'apparent memory' apparent personal memory.

So apparent memory, like apparent perception, is subject to correction. The fundamental principle which we adopt for correcting apparent perception, and for correcting apparent memories of the positions and properties of material bodies, is to select as the most probable hypothesis the simplest hypothesis about what is perceived or remembered which has the consequence that the overwhelming majority of our apparent perceptions and memories are correct. This fundamental principle leads us to adopt more detailed principles with respect to various kinds of bodies—e.g., that metal bodies do not normally change their shape rapidly or randomly and that houses do not normally change their position. We then use these principles to reach particular beliefs, e.g., in the way illustrated with respect to the round-looking metal object. The detailed principles are themselves corrigible and may need to be corrected or to have exceptions made to them, in order that we may continue to hold correct the overwhelming majority of our apparent perceptions and memories.

Analogy would suggest that we ought to deal with apparent memories of who one was in the same kind of way. We find, as we have seen, that in general apparent memory reveals that personal identity goes with brain continuity. It is a simple supposition which has the consequence that the vast majority of our apparent memories are correct, to suppose that in present circumstances brain continuity is a physically necessary condition of personal identity and hence that apparent memories are in error when they are apparently of the deeds of a person who has none of the subject's brain. That will not tell us what is the right answer when brains are split; nor does it cast any doubt on the fact that the ultimate foundation for the belief that personal identity is carried by brain continuity is apparent memory, and that any general failure of the correlation between continuity of apparent memory and continuity of brain must lead us to take brain continuity no longer as evidence of personal identity.[29]

[29]It is for this reason that the general resurrection of the dead (whose brains had been destroyed) is not merely a coherent supposition but one which people could rationally believe to have occurred. If large numbers of people apparently remembered having had the experiences and done the deeds of persons with whom they did not have continuity of brain, it would be right (by the principle of credulity) to believe their apparent memories to be genuine and so to believe that brain continuity was not in those circumstances a necessary condition of personal identity.

So then our general reliance on apparent memory is justified a priori, and it shows us—in the absence of counter-evidence —what was done; and, as Reid (*Essays*, III, ch. 4) put it, 'my memory testifies not only that it was done, but that it was done by me who now remembers it'. Some recent writers have wished to restrict reliance on apparent memory to what was done (and experienced), and to deny that we are justified in relying on it (without further empirical evidence) to show who did and experienced what was done and experienced. Thus Parfit: 'it cannot be a part of what I seem to remember about this experience that I, the person who now seems to remember it, am the person who had this experience' (Parfit 1971b, p. 15). But why on earth not? Experience seems to testify just that— 'that I am the person who had this experience'. It needs a positive argument to show that apparent memory cannot provide the information which it claims to provide—for otherwise, because of the principle of credulity, its testimony must be taken. Parfit rightly points out that there are circumstances in which 'I should cease to assume that my apparent memories must be about my own experiences'. For example, my apparent memories might include apparent memories coinciding with the doings and experiences of two past people, both of whom cannot have been me. Then, for those experiences I should cease to make the assumption that my apparent memories must be about my own experiences. And if that kind of experience was very common indeed, I would cease to rely on apparent memory as evidence of what I did, and merely rely on it as evidence of what was done.

But the same argument applies to any facet of memory. If my apparent memories prove mistaken—as shown by other of my apparent memories and by the evidence of others, ultimately dependent on their apparent memories—in some respect, I cease to rely on them in that respect. If it proves that my memories of faces are unreliable in that I fail by means of them correctly to identify people, I rely on their voices instead. If it proves that I cannot remember what I did more than twenty years ago, I rely in this respect on the memories of others instead. But in the absence of such positive counter-evidence, I have every justification for relying on my memory. If I do not, then, as we saw, I can have no knowledge of the world.

There is a well-known argument[30] which could be deployed to back up Parfit's position, although it is not one which he uses himself. Claims about publicly observable past events involved in claims of apparent memory can be checked. If I claim (because it seems to me that I saw it) that there was a hole in the road yesterday, my claim can be checked, by finding others who apparently remember observing the same thing. But my claim that I myself did or experienced something (e.g., saw the hole) is uncheckable unless my body is evidence of my presence. If I claim to have been in London, my claim is checkable only if the presence of my body in London is evidence of the presence of me in London and its absence is evidence of my absence. So without some sort of physical evidence of a person's presence —and the obvious evidence is that provided by the bodily criterion of personal identity (as amended to a brain criterion)—a person's claims to the effect that he was the person who did and experienced certain things would be uncheckable. So, the argument could go, apparent memory is to be believed where it can be checked—e.g., about physical matters—but not where it cannot be checked; and it can only be checked in its claims about a person's past deeds and experiences if we rely on the bodily criterion of personal identity. Hence the primacy of the bodily criterion (and, through it, of the brain criterion) over the memory criterion.

This argument is not to be accepted. To start with it assumes that if there is no possibility of cross-checking some claim, either that claim has no truth value or at any rate I am not justified in believing it. We have seen in section 3 some reason for doubting any tie of this kind between verifiability and having a truth value, and the assumption that I am not justified in believing something unless there is a possibility of cross-checking is also highly contestable. But let us grant the assumption and note instead that apparent memory can itself be checked by apparent memory. If P_3 at t_3 apparently remembers the deeds and experiences of P_2 at an earlier time t_2 and of P_1 at a yet earlier time t_1, the reliability of this can be checked by investigating whether P_2 apparently remembered the deeds and experiences of P_1. The claim of P_3 to be identical with both P_2 and P_1 is backed up by the evidence of apparent memory that P_2

[30]See Shoemaker 1963, especially pp. 199–202.

and P_1 are identical with each other. This evidence may be obtained by P_3 apparently remembering P_2's apparent memory, or it may be obtained by others if at t_2 P_2 made public memory claims and P_3 did likewise at t_3. In order to make public memory claims, P_2 and P_3 must manifest their presence publicly. They may do this by being embodied and speaking through mouths—and this can happen and be seen to happen without our needing to take for granted that they are embodied in the same bodies. The cross-checkable memory claims would then be evidence that the two persons were the same, without any bodily criterion needing to be employed.

It may be urged by an opponent that there must be at least a short period of embodiment in a continuous body (and so satisfaction of the criterion of sameness of body) for memory claims to be identified as the claims of a single claimant at all—five minutes, say, while through the same mouth a man makes his memory claims. But even that is unnecessary. A voice might speak from mid air, and be reasonably judged to be the voice of the same speaker over a period of time by the sameness of its accent and the grammatical and logical coherence of its message; in those circumstances the principle of simplicity shows us that it is more probable that the noises derive from one speaker than from many.

It follows that the criterion of apparent memory can be used and its deliverances can be checked privately and publicly without any reliance on any bodily criterion. The previous argument to show the primacy of the criterion of apparent memory as a criterion of personal identity stands.

In applying this criterion, we do also bring in, as I noted earlier, sameness of character. If P_2 has the same attitude to the world, habits, reactions, etc., as P_1 that is evidence that he is P_1. Obviously character changes with time; and many people have similar characters. So the criterion hardly provides very strong evidence of personal identity; it needs to be used with other criteria. Again, its satisfaction is evidently a matter of degree. But if it is clearly not satisfied, that is some evidence that two persons are not the same. Now why is sameness of character evidence of personal identity? Is it simply on the observable grounds that as a matter of fact people's characters do not normally change overnight; that is, that when two persons are the same by other criteria, they are generally found to have a similar character or one modified gradually by circumstances in recognizable ways? That is certainly found, but I shall be arguing, this is not mere contingent fact but is quite likely to be found for a priori reasons; and so we must count continuity of character as some slight evidence that two persons at different times are the same, and lack of it as evidence that they are not.

A person's character is his way of viewing the world and his dispositions to kinds of action. That is, it consists of his most general beliefs and purposes. It consists of his beliefs about what people are like (that they are in general benevolent or wise, or, alternatively, wicked and stupid) and his purposes (whether he tries to make all men happy or whether his kindness is limited in amount, and limited to those close to him in creed or blood relationship).

Now a person cannot change his beliefs at will. I cannot choose whether or not to believe that I am now on the moon, or that this year is AD 1066. That belief is passive was a claim of Hume's (*Treatise*, p. 624), but Hume does not bring out that this is a logical matter, not a mere matter of psychology. For if I could change my beliefs at will, I would realize that I was doing this, and so I would realize that my beliefs were in no way dependent on the state of the world, but were simply dependent on my choice. But in that case I could not regard my beliefs as in any way corresponding to the facts; and so I could not really believe them. Only if I think of my beliefs as forced upon me by the facts will I believe them.

A person's beliefs will change only if he is presented with new evidence, or if he comes to assess the old evidence in a different way. New evidence takes time to accumulate, and it needs a lot of new evidence to overthrow old beliefs, if your criteria for assessing evidence remain the same. If all the clues show, by your present criteria, that Jones did the murder, it will need a lot of new evidence to overthrow them. However strong the counter-evidence, it will be suspect unless it accumulates; if Jones produces an apparently cast-iron alibi, that alibi will in the light of your other evidence immediately be suspect. What goes for such low-level beliefs goes, far more evidently, for very general beliefs—no one piece of evidence is going to change your view of human nature, given your present criteria for assessing evidence. Could not these criteria suddenly change? No. I could not change them at will for the reason given above. And if I suddenly found myself one morning with a new set of standards for assessing evidence, I would be struck by their disconsonance with my former standards. And unless I could provide some justification for the new standards, the arbitrariness of the standards would inevitably strike me; and if it did, I would lack confidence in my standards and so not really believe the claims which those standards supported. Justification would consist in showing that the new standards were an improved version of the old ones (e.g., with inconsistencies and awkwardnesses removed) or were justified by the old ones in the light of some observed evidence. By whatever route there must be continuity in a person's standards for assessing evidence, and so in his beliefs about the world. There must be continuity between a person's beliefs one day and his beliefs the next day; only gradual change is possible.

But surely a person's purposes can change overnight? Cannot conversion change the whole direction of a person's life? Yes, but this is (a priori) not too likely, for the following reason. In so far as a person believes some action to be good, he will in the absence of strong desire diverting him, do the action. A person's beliefs about which actions are good make him inclined to do those actions. He may yield to temptation to do otherwise, or resist that temptation; on that the choice is his. But the belief gives him the inclination and so produces some likelihood that he will follow it. Since beliefs can only change slowly, this makes it quite likely that the same will hold of purposes. There are, of course, exceptions of a heroic or lamentable kind—the man who suddenly resolves to resist all temptation and keeps his resolves; or the man who suddenly decides to yield to all temptation. But belief does give a man an inclination to certain kinds of conduct; and that fact makes it hard for a man to act in a completely different way another day.

So a person's beliefs cannot change suddenly, and because of this there are reasons why sudden change of purpose is none too likely. Hence character is very likely to exhibit some continuity. But in which respects it will show continuity, and in which respects change and to what degree, is none too predictable. Further, the above arguments depend on a crucial assumption that the person remembers correctly (in broad outline) his past beliefs. The arguments were designed to show that it was unlikely that his views and purposes would change overnight from those which he believed himself to have previously. My arguments do not rule out a man totally forgetting all his past life, his past standards for assessing evidence, his past views on right and wrong; and simply starting again. Maybe a man could indeed bathe in the waters of Lethe. Nor do they rule out a man having a false memory of his past life as a man with certain views and purposes, and a present character continuous with that of his imagined past life but discontinuous with that of his actual past life.

But what my arguments do count against is a man having an apparent memory of his past life and yet a character totally discontinuous with that former character apparently remembered. For belief must greatly influence character. An apparent sharp discontinuity of character between a person as he now is and that person as he apparently remembers himself to have been must count slightly against the reliability in this instance of the criterion of apparent memory; and, conversely, continuity of such character must count in favour of the reliability in this instance of the criterion of apparent memory.

The outcome of this section is that although personal identity is not constituted by any of the kinds of evidence which I have discussed, it is apparent memory which provides the most direct evidence of it. With apparent memory will be expected to go some continuity of character, and evidence of this adds to or subtracts from the evidence of apparent memory. Continuity of brain is an indirect criterion of personal identity; we use it only because of the almost universal coincidence of its results with those given by the criterion of apparent memory. That, however, does make it a very reliable criterion, to be used in particular cases in preference even to the criterion of apparent memory. In the absence of frequent brain transplants, continuity of body is strong evidence of continuity of brain; and similarity of appearance (backed up by such physiological tests as fingerprints and blood groups) is strong evidence of continuity of body. Such is the complicated web of criteria by which we make our judgements about personal identity.

The apparent memories which provide the primary evidence

of personal identity are apparent memories of what one did oneself, and the argument for relying on them in no way presupposed any bodily or brain continuity of one's present self with one's previous self. Nor did it presuppose that if one cannot remember something one didn't do it. On the contrary memory is a device for discovering what happened (including what one did oneself) independently of whether one can remember it. The argument argued, rather, that one's own past deeds and experiences were data often revealed (albeit fallibly) by memory, and that one has done the deed or had the experience was not something further analysable. (I argued similarly in section 3 that the continuity of oneself over a short period was often a datum of present experience.) This view fits perfectly with the dualist theory which affirms the unanalysability of personal identity in terms of empirical data. The dualist theory can indeed account for our reliance on the criterion of apparent memory, and thereby on the other indirect criteria.

Personal Identity
A Materialist's Account

SYDNEY SHOEMAKER

Acknowledgements

This essay develops ideas suggested in my earlier writings, especially 'Persons and their Pasts' (*American Philosophical Quarterly*, 1970) and 'Identity, Properties and Causality' (*Midwest Studies in Philosophy*, 1979). A more remote ancestor is my book *Self-Knowledge and Self-Identity* (Ithaca, 1963). I am grateful to all of those, including countless students, whose criticisms, questions and comments have helped me clarify my thinking on this subject. I especially thank Carl Ginet and Alan Sidelle, for helpful comments on my contributions to this volume.

1 Introduction

From earliest times people have found intelligible, and sometimes believable, the idea that persons are capable of surviving
death, either in disembodied form or through bodily resurrection or reincarnation. And many a piece of popular fiction relies
on the idea that a person might have different bodies at different
times. We are also familiar, both from fiction and from the
annals of psychiatric medicine, with the idea of two or more
distinct 'personalities' successively manifesting themselves in
one and the same body. Yet another such idea is that two
distinct minds or consciousnesses might simultaneously inhabit
the same body—and recent studies of 'split-brain patients' have
suggested to some investigators not only that this is conceivable
but that it actually happens.[1] One way of raising the problem of
personal identity is by asking whether, or to what extent, such
ideas are coherent, and what it is about the nature of personal
identity, or our concept of it, which permits, or forbids, such
envisioned departures from the normal course of events.

The problem of personal identity can be viewed as an aspect
of the 'mind–body problem'. For a variety of reasons we are
inclined to resist the view, so strongly suggested by the current
scientific world view, that mental states and processes are
nothing over and above certain highly complex physical and
chemical processes. One reason is the 'special access' we have to
our own mental states. One comes to have knowledge of these
states without observing, or gathering evidence about, the
physical states of one's own body; and possession of the
knowledge seems compatible with total ignorance of one's own
inner physiological states, and, more generally, the condition of
one's body. And if one reflects on what one knows in having this
self-knowledge—the existence of intentional states like believing that Argentina's inflation rate is higher than Brazil's, and
qualitative states like seeing blue and having an itch—it is
difficult at best to see how this could be reducible to any facts
about one's behaviour or neurophysiology. Puzzlement about
the nature of mental states is bound to give rise to puzzlement

[1]See Nagel 1979.

about the nature of persons, the pre-eminent subjects of such states. And this in turn manifests itself in puzzlement about personal identity—for a central part of understanding the nature of a kind of things (like persons) is understanding the identity conditions for things of that sort. The considerations that make it seem that mental states cannot be physical states also make it seem that persons cannot simply be physical bodies, and that personal identity must consist in something other than bodily identity.

Among the things to which persons have a 'special access' are facts about their own identity over time; they have this in their memory knowledge of their own past histories. One's memory knowledge of one's own past differs strikingly from one's knowledge, including memory knowledge, of the past histories of other persons. If I claim to remember *you* doing something yesterday, it is at least a theoretical possibility that my claim is in error, not because my memory is mistaken, but because the person I remember doing that thing is not you but someone who looks just like you and whom I have misidentified as you. But if I claim to remember that I did such-and-such yesterday, it is absurd to suppose that I could be mistaken in *that* way. And whatever may be said of my judgements about the identity of others, it is certainly not the case that I ground such judgements about myself on evidence of bodily identity. Here again the nature of self-knowledge raises questions about personal identity, in part by calling into question the natural view that the identity of a person is simply the identity of a living human body.

A rather different source of perplexity about personal identity has to do with the special concern persons have for their own continued existence and their own future welfare. Imagine that a wizard demonstrates to you his ability to reduce any object to a pile of dust by a wave of his wand and then, with another wave, to create an exact duplicate of that thing out of another pile of dust. If one really believes that he can do this, one probably would not be too averse to letting him do it to one's kitchen stove. But only a monster would offer his wife or child as a subject for the wizard's trick, and only a madman (or a suicide) would offer himself. Or so it initially strikes us. Our concern for personal identity, the kind of importance it has for us, seems totally different in kind from the concern we have for the identity of other sorts of things. And this is linked to the special concern each person has for his or her own future welfare. It is this that gives point to many of our moral, social and legal practices, and explains the significance they attach to considerations of personal identity. If a person does an action, it is that same person who can later be held responsible for the action, and whom it is appropriate to punish or reward for doing it. If someone buys something, it is that person who is subsequently entitled to the use of the item purchased. These principles, which are constitutive of the institutions of punishment and property and the concept of moral responsibility, are intelligible only against the background of a conception of human motivation in which a central role is played by the special concern each person has for his own future well-being.

An account of personal identity ought to make intelligible the knowledge we have of personal identity, including the special access each of us has, in memory, to his own identity, and it ought to make intelligible the special sort of importance personal identity has for us. It ought also to cohere with the rest of what we know about the world. In my own view, this last requirement means that an account of personal identity ought to be compatible with a naturalistic, or materialistic, account of mind. To a large extent, the mind–body problem, including the problem of personal identity, arises because of considerations that create the appearance that no naturalistic account could be true; and I think that solving the problem has got to consist in large part in dispelling that appearance (while acknowledging and explaining the facts that give rise to it). Finally, our account of personal identity must be compatible with the logical principles that govern the notion of identity itself. It is to these that we now turn.

2 The Concept of Identity

Logicians characterize identity as an 'equivalence relation', meaning by this a relation that is transitive (if a has it to b, and b has it to c, then a has it to c), symmetrical (if a has it to b, b has it to a), and reflexive (everything has it to itself). It is marked off from other equivalence relationships by its conformity to Leibniz's Law (the principle of the indiscernibility of identicals), which says that if a is identical to b, then whatever is true of a is true of b, and conversely. Identity is even more briefly characterizable as the relation which everything has, necessarily, to itself, and which nothing has to anything other than itself (but the last clause makes this definition circular, since it means 'and which nothing has to anything not identical to itself').

It is important to distinguish the relation of identity we are here concerned with from another relation that bears the same name. In the baggage claim areas of some airports are signs reading 'Careful: many suitcases are identical'.[2] This is a perfectly correct use of 'identical', but not in the sense of it relevant to the problem of personal identity. In the airport sign, 'identical' means 'exactly alike'; it expresses what is sometimes called 'qualitative identity' (or 'qualitative sameness'). This must be distinguished from the sense of 'identical' in which it means 'one and the same', and expresses 'numerical identity' (or 'numerical sameness'). It is the latter, the sense of 'identical' in which 'identical twins' (and identical suitcases) are not identical, that concerns us here.

Confusion of these two senses of 'identical' (and 'same') is one source of the idea that identity over time is incompatible with change. If something changes, then in some respect it is no longer the same as it was; the thing at the earlier time and the thing at the later time are not 'identical'. Indeed, we may seem to be driven into contradiction here: if I say 'A is not the same as *it* was', I seem to imply identity with the pronoun 'it' while denying it by saying 'not the same'. But the contradiction is only

[2] Reported by Saul Kripke, in a lecture.

apparent; the identity that is implied is numerical identity, while that which is denied is qualitative identity. Change is incompatible with qualitative identity between the successive states of the changing thing; but it not only allows, but logically requires, that the successive states be states of numerically the same thing.

Another source of the view that identity over time is incompatible with change is a misunderstanding of Leibniz's Law. If a leaf is green in the summer and yellow in the fall, then in a certain sense something is true of it in the summer which is not true of it in the fall, and vice versa. But this is no violation of Leibniz's Law. If A is a leaf in the summer and B is a leaf in the fall, what Leibniz's Law holds to follow from 'A is identical to B' is not that if A is green in the summer then B is green in the fall; it is rather that if A is green in the summer then B is green in the summer (and if B is yellow in the fall, A is yellow in the fall). More generally, it tells us that whatever property A has at a time, B must have at that time, and conversely; and this is entirely compatible with A (=B) having different properties at different times.

More common than the view that identity over time is incompatible with any sort of change is the view that it is incompatible with one particular sort of change—change of composition. This stems in part from the confusions already mentioned, but has another source as well. If over a period of time some of the molecules in a tree are replaced by others, then in one sense we no longer have the same 'substance' as we had before. Now there is a well established philosophical sense of 'substance', going back to Aristotle, in which a tree *is* a substance. And to say in *this* sense that we no longer have the same substance is to say (in the case at hand) that we no longer have the same tree—which is the view Bishop Butler took of the case in which, over time, all of the matter in a tree is replaced.[3] But surely we should distinguish these senses of 'substance'. When we say that we no longer have the same substance in this case, what counts as a substance is a particular portion or quantity of matter. But it is not in *this* sense that a tree is a substance. The tree is, at a particular time, composed of a particular portion of matter, but that is not to say that it is

[3]pp. 100–1 in Perry 1975a.

identical to that portion of matter and that it could not at some later time be composed of some quite different matter. And of course we regularly do take things like trees to survive the gradual (and in the case of things like rivers and waterfalls, not so gradual) replacement of the matter of which they are composed. To argue that such replacement is impossible on the grounds that being the same tree requires being the same substance either equivocates on the word 'substance' or begs the question. I think that we can see from this that it is either false or vacuous to say that the identity of things like trees consists in their being or having the same substance; it is false if 'substance' means 'portion of stuff', and vacuous if 'substance' means 'persisting subject of properties' (for then the claim comes to: being the same tree consists in being the same tree).

Some writers like to speak of the identity over time of a person or a table as consisting in the occurrence of a succession of momentary 'person-stages' or 'table-stages' that are related to one another in certain ways. (Some speak of 'time-slices' rather than of 'stages'). So, for example, if I say 'The table I am sitting at now is the table I was sitting at yesterday', I am asserting a relation to hold between a table-stage occurring now and one occurring yesterday. But it is important to be clear that the relation I assert to hold between the stages is not itself identity; today's table-stage and yesterday's table-stage cannot be the same, since stages are individuated by the times at which they occur. Let us pretend, for the moment, that different table-stages are stages of one and the same table if they belong to a single spatiotemporally continuous succession of table-stages—or, for short, if they are 'table-linked'. Here we can say, following John Perry, that the relation of being table-linked is the *unity relation* for tables.[4] The unity relation is not identity; it is rather the relation that holds between different table-stages when they are stages of one and the same table. Nevertheless, to specify the unity relation for tables is to say what the identity over time of tables consists in. And one way of formulating the problem of personal identity is to ask what the unity relation for persons is, i.e., what is the relation between person-stages occurring at different times, in virtue of which they are stages of one and the same person.

[4]See Perry 1975b.

What sort of thing is a 'person-stage' or 'table-stage'? Some philosophers who use this terminology think of persons and other continuants as four-dimensional objects which have temporal as well as spatial parts. For them momentary stages will be either temporally very small parts of continuants or temporally unextended cross-sections of them taken at particular moments of time. But one need not be committed to the four-dimensional view of ordinary continuants in order to use this terminology. Person-stages can be thought of as 'temporal slices', not of persons, but of the histories or careers of persons. One might think of a momentary stage as a set of property instantiations; if C is a continuant existing at time t, and P is the set of properties possessed by C at t, then C's stage at t will be the set consisting of the instantiations in C at t of the properties in P. Or one can think of a momentary stage as an ordered pair consisting of a thing and a time; C's stage at t will be just the ordered pair $\langle C, t \rangle$.

Questions about identity over time can be said to be questions about the *diachronic* unity of continuants of some kind, e.g., persons or tables. Questions can also be raised about the *synchronic* unity of such things. In some cases the latter are questions about 'identity across space'; for example, if we were concerned (with Heraclitus) about the identity of rivers we might ask why it is that the river (or river part) at Minneapolis and that at New Orleans count as (parts of) the same river. In the case of persons, questions about synchronic unity are more likely to be asked about momentary experiences and other mental states than about spatial parts. The question will be: in virtue of what do different experiences or mental states occurring at the same time count as belonging to one and the same person? This is sometimes posed as the problem of the 'unity of consciousness'. A useful term for the unity relation for persons (both diachronic and synchronic) is Bertrand Russell's term 'copersonal'.[5]

There is a tradition, going back to Bishop Butler, of holding that personal identity is indefinable and unanalysable, that no non-trivial account can be given of the identity conditions for persons, and that personal identity does not 'consist' in anything. Butler (and likewise Thomas Reid) seemed to think

[5]Russell, 'The Philosophy of Logical Atomism', p. 277.

that this is a consequence of personal identity being identity in a 'strict and philosophical sense'—as contrasted with the 'loose and popular sense' he believed to be invoked in our ascription of identity over time to such things as trees and ships. There are contemporary philosophers who think that Butler was right. But we will begin with the working assumption that an account of personal identity can be given. Indeed, we will begin with the view Butler was primarily attacking, that of John Locke.

3 The Memory Theory

Locke's central thesis was that personal identity consists, not in sameness of substance, but in 'sameness of consciousness'.[6] It is by no means uncontroversial what Locke meant by this. But it is clear enough that 'consciousness' for Locke includes memory, and that it is primarily memory he has in mind when he speaks of consciousness in his discussion of personal identity. Rightly or wrongly, Locke has been taken as the founder of the view that the identity over time of a person consists in facts about memory and the capacity to remember. He seems, in fact, to have held a fairly extreme version of that view: that a person A existing at a time t_2 is the same as a person B existing at an earlier time t_1 if and only if A remembers, or 'can remember', at t_2 actions or experiences of B occurring at t_1.

Before we consider the objections that have been raised against this view we must try to understand its initial appeal. We have already noted (section 1) that the way a person knows of his own past on the basis of memory is different from that in which he knows of the past of any other person. When I claim to remember *your* doing such-and-such yesterday, a question can arise whether the person I remember doing that thing was really you, and not someone else who looked like you (and this is so even if the accuracy of my memory of the incident is conceded); when I claim to remember *my* doing such-and-such a thing yesterday, no such question can arise. There seems to be a way of remembering past experiences and actions—I call it 'remembering from the inside'—such that if someone remembers X (an action or experience) in that way, it follows that X was an experience or action of that person.[7] Already, then, we seem to have an intimate connection between memory and personal identity: the person who remembers from the inside must be identical to the person who earlier had the remembered experience or did the remembered action. What I am calling 'remembering from the inside' is the kind of memory a person

[6]Locke's *Essay* was first published in 1690, but the chapter on 'Identity and Diversity' was added in the second edition, which appeared in 1694.
[7]See Shoemaker 1970a, p. 180.

has of a past action when he remembers *doing* it, or of an experience when he remembers *having* it. But there also seems to be a more general connection between personal identity and memory which is not restricted to remembering from the inside: if someone remembers any event whatever, he must be identical to one of those who witnessed that event, or otherwise knew of it in a direct way, at the time of its occurrence. I can remember *that* the Battle of Hastings occurred in 1066, but no one now alive can be said to remember the Battle of Hastings.

It is not only from the first-person point of view that the memory theory, and the allied view that personal identity is independent of bodily identity, can seem attractive. Locke remarks that 'should the soul of a prince, carrying with it the consciousness of the prince's past life, enter and inform the body of a cobbler, as soon deserted by his own soul, everyone sees he would be the same person with the prince, accountable only for the prince's actions' (Locke, *Essay Concerning Human Understanding*, ed. P. H. Nidditch, p. 340). It is easy enough to develop this into a case in which we could have rather compelling evidence, based on considerations having to do with memory, that someone had 'changed bodies'. For those who are sceptical about 'souls', it may help to imagine a case in which what are switched are not souls but brains. Suppose, then, that by a surgical blunder (of rather staggering proportions!) Brown's brain gets into Robinson's head.[8] When the resulting person, call him 'Brownson', regains consciousness, he claims to be Brown, and exhibits detailed knowledge of Brown's past life, always reporting Brown's deeds and experiences in the first person. It is hard to resist the conclusion that we, viewing the case from the outside, ought to accept Brownson's claim to be Brown, precisely on the basis of the evidence that he remembers Brown's life from the inside. This gives prima facie support to the Lockean view that personal identity consists in part in facts having to do with memory.

A variety of objections have been raised against the memory theory, and some of these are clearly telling against the version

---

[8]See Shoemaker 1963, pp. 22–5.

apparently held by Locke. What I want to do next is to consider how Locke's view might be modified to meet these objections, with a view to seeing whether a modified version of it can provide an acceptable theory of personal identity.

4 Objections and Revisions

The most famous objections to Locke's account are those raised in the eighteenth century by Bishop Butler and Thomas Reid. Butler charged that the account is circular: 'one should really think it self-evident, that consciousness of personal identity presupposes, and therefore cannot constitute, personal identity, any more than knowledge, in any other case, can constitute truth, which it presupposes' (p. 100, in Perry 1975a). Reid charged that the account is self-contradictory, and sought to show this with his 'brave officer' example.[9] At a certain time a boy is flogged for robbing an orchard. Years later the same person, now a young officer, performs a valiant deed in battle, remembering still his boyhood flogging. Many years later our man is an elderly general, who remembers the valiant deed in battle, but no longer remembers the flogging. Reid charges that on Locke's theory the old general both is and is not the same person as the small boy; he is the same because he is identical to the young officer who is identical to the small boy (and because identity is transitive); he is not the same because he has no memory of the flogging (and, let us suppose, has no memory at all of that period of the boy's life).

Let us begin with Reid's objection. Plainly the objection is decisive if the memory theory makes it a necessary and sufficient condition of someone's being the person who did a past action that he should remember that action. A defender of Locke might try to parry the objection by pointing out that what Locke requires for personal identity is that one *can* remember the action of the earlier person, not that one *does* remember it, and that it is plausible that under some possible circumstances (hypnosis, psychoanalysis) Reid's old general would remember the childhood incident, and so in that sense 'can' remember it. What Reid says, however, is that the old general had 'absolutely lost consciousness of the flogging', and it seems plausible to take the 'absolutely' as implying that the memory was lost without any possibility of recall. The example still seems possible under that interpretation.

[9] pp. 114–15 in Perry 1975a.

Plainly the simple Lockean theory must be revised. The standard revision to meet this difficulty is most conveniently put in the person-stage terminology. Take the simple Lockean theory to hold that two person-stages belong to the same person if and only if the later contains memories (from the inside) of experiences, etc., contained in the earlier one. Here we should allow that one's current person-stage contains a memory of something even if one has temporarily forgotten that thing, as long as one has the potentiality of remembering it. In such a case the stage will retain a 'memory trace' that is the basis of that potentiality. Let us say that two person-stages that are so related are 'memory- connected'. The revised Lockean account says that the unity relation for persons is not the relation of being memory-connected but the 'ancestral' of this relation. This comes to saying that two stages belong to the same person if and only if they are the end-points of a series of stages such that each member of the series is memory-connected with the preceding member. One such series consists of the stage of the boy at the time of his flogging, the stage of the young officer at the time of his valiant deed, and a stage of the old general at a time at which he remembers the valiant deed but not the flogging. What this account makes necessary for identity with a 'past self' is not that one remember the actions and experiences of that past self but that one have 'memory continuity' with that past self—memory continuity consisting in the occurrence of a chain of memory-connected person-stages of the sort just described.[10]

Rather than address myself directly to Butler's objection, which seems to me to attack something Locke never said, I shall consider some circularity objections, perhaps descendants of Butler's, which seem to me more fundamental. It is arguable, first of all, that, far from personal identity being definable in terms of memory, memory must be defined in terms of personal identity. A definition of what it is for a person S to remember a particular event E could be expected to include the provisions (1) that S now has a state (which could be dispositional) which could be called an apparent memory, and (2) that the content of that apparent memory 'matches' in an appropriate way the

[10]For more precise formulations of such modified Lockean accounts, see Grice 1941, and Perry 1975b.

nature of the past event E. But it is obvious that these conditions are not sufficient; if your first haircut was exactly like mine, I do not automatically remember yours in remembering mine. The obvious remedy is to supplement conditions (1) and (2) with the additional requirement (3) that S was appropriately related to E at the time of its occurrence, i.e., he witnessed it, underwent it (if it was a haircut), performed it (if it was an action), and so on. But if the definition of 'S remembers E' contains condition (3), then we cannot without circularity use the notion of event memory to define personal identity, since (3) implicitly invokes the notion of personal identity—it implies that the person S who now satisfies condition (1) is *the same person* as someone in the past who was involved in a certain way with event E. It may further be argued (and this is perhaps closer to what Butler had in mind) that the particular sort of memory I have called 'remembering from the inside' cannot be characterized without the use of the notion of personal identity. For it may be claimed that to say that someone remembers *doing* an action, or *having* an experience, is elliptical for saying that he remembers *himself* doing the action or having the experience, and that for this reason these locutions (and the notion of 'remembering from the inside' which is explained in terms of them) cannot without circularity be used in an account of personal identity.

The first step towards answering these objections is to see that the addition of condition (3) to conditions (1) and (2) does not give us a sufficient condition for the truth of 'S remembers E'. There can be memory illusions, and it is perfectly possible for an illusory memory to happen to correspond to something that happened to its subject in the past. For example, a hypnotist induces in me an apparent memory of having visited Yellowstone Park as a child, and it just so happens (unbeknownst to the hypnotist) that I did visit Yellowstone Park as a child, but have completely forgotten about it. The case I want is not one in which the hypnotist brings to consciousness a latent memory which was already present, but rather one in which my apparent memory of the visit to Yellowstone is entirely due to the hypnotist's suggestion, and not at all due to my childhood visit to the Park—i.e., it is such that I would have had the very same apparent memory even if I had never visited Yellowstone.

In this case I clearly do not remember the visit to Yellowstone, even though conditions (1)–(3) are all satisfied. What this brings out is that the notion of memory is a *causal* notion; it is a necessary condition of a person's remembering a past event that his apparent memory of that event should be caused, in an appropriate way, by that event itself.[11]

What this may seem to call for is the replacement of condition (3) by something like this: (3′) S's apparent memory (mentioned in (1)) was caused, in an appropriate way, by his experiencing (or otherwise being involved in) E at the time of its occurrence. Of course, (3′) implicitly invokes the notion of personal identity in the same way that (3) does, and so does not get us out of the circularity. But it is not obvious that we cannot formulate the causal requirement, and make it do the work done by (3) and (3′), without invoking the notion of personal identity. The requirement might be: (3″) S's apparent memory (mentioned in (1)) was caused, in an appropriate way, by someone's experiencing (or otherwise being involved in) E at the time of its occurrence. Replacing 'his' (or 'S's') with 'someone's' eliminates the circularity—or rather, it does so *if* the notion of 'being caused in an appropriate way' can be spelled out without invoking the notion of personal identity.

That some such phrase as 'in an appropriate way' is needed in the causal condition can be seen from a modification of my Yellowstone Park example. Suppose that at some time in my life a traumatic experience completely obliterated my memory of that incident. Prior to that time, however, I told someone about the visit, on the basis of the accurate memory I then had of it, and that person subsequently told the hypnotist about it. What the hypnotist did was instil in me an apparent memory which corresponded to the account he was given of my visit, an account which originally came from me. But he did not restore or revive my memory—it was irretrievably gone. Rather, he instilled in me a memory illusion which he could just as easily have instilled in someone who had never been to Yellowstone. Yet my apparent memory not only 'matches' the past event but is traceable back to it by a causal chain that goes through the hypnotist and his informant back to my earlier memory of

[11]See Deutscher and Martin 1966.

the event, and via that back to the event itself. Here we have a causal connection, but not one of the 'appropriate sort'.

If 'causal connection of the appropriate sort' could only be explained as meaning something like 'connection via a causal chain that does not go outside the states of a single person', obviously (3″) would invoke the notion of personal identity as much as (3) did, and the circularity objection would stand. However, there are reasons for thinking that this is not so.

One thing that seems clear is that we can *know* that there is a causal connection of the appropriate sort, and therefore that a person remembers a past event, without *first* knowing the relevant fact of personal identity (i.e., that the rememberer is identical to someone who experienced the remembered past event). For consider again the brain transfer example described earlier. If Brownson does indeed manifest apparent memories of Brown's past life, the fact that he has Brown's brain would seem to provide sufficient reason for thinking that these memories are 'caused in an appropriate way' by Brown's past actions and experiences, and thus that Brownson really does remember those actions and experiences, which in turn can serve as a basis for saying that Brownson is Brown. If we had to settle the question of identity prior to discovering whether Brownson's apparent memories really are memories of Brown's life, we could not use an affirmative answer to the latter question as a basis for an affirmative answer to the former. Yet it seems that we can do this.

Moreover, there seem to be conceivable cases in which we can have the appropriate sort of causal connection for memory in the absence of identity between the rememberer and the person who experienced the remembered event. It may seem that if such cases are possible, they get us out of the circularity problem only at the cost of falsifying the memory theory; but we will see that the memory theory can easily be modified so as to accommodate such cases. The possible cases I have in mind are what have been called cases of 'fission'—cases (entirely imaginary, of course) in which a person somehow divides into two persons. The most realistic such case is one described by David Wiggins.[12] He imagines a complex brain-transplant in

---

[12]Wiggins 1967, p. 53.

which the two hemispheres of someone's brain are transplanted, separately, into the skulls of two different bodies. The result of the operation, we will suppose, is that both offshoots have memories from the inside of the life of the original person. It would be difficult to maintain that each offshoot is identical to the original person, since plainly they are not identical to each other (after the operation they go their separate ways, and soon can be distinguished on psychological grounds as well as by spatial location and physical properties).[13] And it would seem arbitrary to suggest that one is identical to the original person and the other not.[14] Yet it would be hard to deny that the apparent memories both have of the original person's life are genuine memories, and are related to events in that past life by causal connections 'of the appropriate sort'.

It is easy to see how the Lockean memory theory can be modified to allow for this case. We will simply say that memory continuity is sufficient for personal identity as long as there is no 'branching' in the chain of person-stages—where the fission case illustrates what is meant by 'branching'. I will have more to say about the fission example later on. Its importance here is that its possibility seems to count against the claim that the 'appropriate sort' of causal connection for memory can only be characterized as one that involves personal identity, and thus helps to defuse the circularity objection.

The fission case also helps with the objection that memory 'from the inside' can only be characterized as the sort of memory a person has of his own past, and thus that any attempt to define personal identity in terms of it will be circular. If the offshoots in the fission case are not identical to the original person, then their memories of that person's actions and experiences will not be memories of their own actions and experiences. Yet, for all that, they will remember those actions and experiences in the way in which normally one can remember only one's own actions and experiences.

[13]But see Perry 1972 and Lewis 1976 for attempts to circumvent this difficulty.

[14]It is really only for materialists (or anti-dualists) that this would be arbitrary. A believer in indivisible immaterial souls would of course insist that at most one of the offshoots would inherit the soul of the original person.

This is remembering from the inside, and it is something which in principle we can have in the absence of personal identity.

It will be seen that I have abandoned the claims, tentatively made in section 3, that it is necessarily the case that one can remember a past event only if one was a witness to it, and can remember a past experience or action from the inside only if it was an experience or action of one's own. An alternative approach, which differs only verbally from that presented here, is to hold on to these claims and to introduce a technical term, 'quasi-remember', for the notion defined in terms of conditions (1), (2) and (3″). The definition of personal identity will then be in terms of quasi-remembering (quasi-memory) rather than in terms of remembering (memory). Remembering will now be a special case of quasi-remembering; it will be quasi-remembering in which the rememberer is identical to the person who experienced or underwent the quasi-remembered event.[15]

There remains, however, an objection to the memory theory which is simpler and more direct than those considered so far. This is just that it seems conceivable that someone should survive total amnesia, total loss of memory.[16] If that happens, there will be no chain of memory-connected person-stages going from stages prior to the onset of the amnesia to stages subsequent to it. So this possibility counts against the modified Lockean theory as well as against the simple theory.

We must be careful here about what is meant by 'amnesia'. What is ordinarily meant is a total or partial loss of memory which can be recovered from; it is a condition that it treatable by hypnosis and in other ways. The possibility of total amnesia in this sense is no threat to the memory theory, since the amnesia victim can be presumed to retain memories in latent form. What is needed to refute the memory theory is the possibility of what might be called 'philosophical amnesia', i.e., the irreversible loss of all memory of the past.

But in addition to distinguishing different sorts of amnesia we must distinguish different sorts of memory. What we have meant by memory up until now is what is sometimes called 'event memory'—memory of particular events in the past. But there are other sorts of memory that are equally important.

[15]This was my approach in Shoemaker 1970a.
[16]See Wiggins 1980, p. 167 and pp. 176–7.

There is 'factual memory'—remembering *that* De Soto discovered the Mississippi River, *that* sulphuric acid is H_2SO_4, *that* there will be an eclipse tomorrow. There is remembering how to do something—ride a bicycle, tie a bow tie, etc. There is remembering the meaning of 'soigner', the smell of lilacs, and so on. If the claim that philosophical amnesia is possible means that someone can suffer total and irreversible loss of memories of all past events, so that from a certain time onwards the person has, and can have, no memory of events prior to that time, then I think that we must allow that this is possible. But if 'philosophical amnesia' is taken to mean total and irretrievable loss of all memories of all kinds, then the claim that a person can survive such amnesia is far more questionable. For what we are now imagining is something close to what has been called a 'brain zap'—the total destruction of all of the effects of the person's past experience, learning, reasoning, deliberation, and so on.[17] Whether it is physiologically possible that a human body should survive a brain zap and remain alive and capable of realizing a mental life of a human sort seems questionable, to say the least. But let us suppose this is possible. Suppose that in a terrible accident a person suffers brain damage amounting to a total brain zap, and that somehow the surgeons manage to repair the brain in such a way that its possessor is able to start again, as it were, as if he were an infant. Eventually that body is again the body of someone with the mental life of a mature human being; but it is someone whose conception of the world, along with his personality and character, was formed by the experience of that body since the time of the accident and the reconstitution of the brain. It is anything but obvious that this person would be the person who had the body prior to the accident. So if total amnesia means this sort of brain zap, it is far from uncontroversial—indeed it seems just false—that it is something a person could survive.

But perhaps a total and irreversible loss of all memories need not amount to a brain zap. A person's personality, character, tastes, interests and so on are the product (at least in part) of his past experience, and it is not obvious that the loss of all memories would necessarily involve the loss of all such traits as

[17]Perry 1976b, p. 421.

these. To be sure, to a certain extent personality and character traits do seem inseparable from memories of certain kinds. It is hard to see how someone's pacifism could survive his loss of all of his beliefs about the effects of warfare. However, let us assume that there are some traits of personality that could, at least in principle, survive a total and irreversible loss of all memories. If that is so, such a loss of memory would not necessarily amount to a total brain zap; and then it becomes more plausible to suppose that such a loss of memory is something a person could survive—in which case the memory theory, even as revised, is false.

5 Personal Identity as Psychological Continuity

This requires us to consider something we would have had to consider anyhow, namely the role *vis-à-vis* personal identity of kinds of psychological continuity other than memory continuity—I mean continuity with respect to the sorts of traits just mentioned: interests, tastes, talents, and traits of personality and character. Let us return to the Brown–Brownson case. If Brownson's possession of Brown's brain makes it plausible that he will have memories from the inside of Brown's past life, it makes it equally plausible that he will resemble Brown psychologically in all of the ways one expects a person on one day to resemble himself as he was the day before, and this resemblance would certainly be part of our reason for regarding Brownson as the same person as Brown. Suppose just for the moment that while Brownson's memories-from-the-inside are all of Brown's past, his personality and character traits are those of the old Robinson; I think that in this case (which would be physiologically unintelligible, and perhaps psychologically unintelligible as well) we would be much more hesitant about identifying Brownson with Brown.

We know, of course, that different people can share personality and character traits. And this may seem a reason for saying that Brownson's similarity to Brown with respect to such traits could not be part of what constitutes his identity with Brown, even though it might be evidence for it. This may suggest that, conceptually speaking, memory continuity is much more intimately related to personal identity than is similarity and continuity of personality. But all of this ignores the fact that what we have in the Brown–Brownson case is not merely similarity of personality and character. Brownson does not merely have the same personality traits as Brown did; he has those traits *because* Brown's life was such as to lead him to acquire such traits. The fact that Brownson has Brown's brain gives us reason to suppose that there is a relationship of causal or counterfactual dependence between Brownson's traits subsequent to the brain transfer and Brown's traits prior to it—we have reason to think that if Brown's traits had been different,

Brownson's traits would have been different in corresponding ways. It is precisely when the circumstances are such that evidence of similarity is evidence of such a causal or counterfactual dependence that evidence of similarity is evidence of identity. Indeed, it is for the same reason that the nature of Brownson's memories is evidence that he is Brown; we have reason to think that if Brown's life had been different, Brownson's memories would have been correspondingly different, and thus that Brownson's memories are causally and counterfactually dependent on Brown's past life. Thus the status of similarity and continuity of personality traits as evidence of personal identity seems no different than that of memory continuity; both are evidence only in so far as they include, or are evidence for, causal relations between earlier and later states.

Henceforth I shall use the term 'psychological continuity' to cover both of these sorts of causally grounded continuity. The memory continuity account of personal identity thus gives way to a more general psychological continuity account.[18] Memory continuity is now seen as just a special case of psychological continuity, and it is in psychological continuity that personal identity is now held to consist. Reverting to the 'person-stage' terminology, two person-stages will be directly connected, psychologically, if the later of them contains a psychological state (a memory impression, personality trait, etc.) which stands in the appropriate relation of causal dependence to a state contained in the earlier one; and two stages belong to the same person if and only if (1) they are connected by a series of stages such that each member of the series is directly connected, psychologically, to the immediately preceding member, and (2) no such series of stages which connects them 'branches' at any point, i.e., contains a member which is directly connected, psychologically, to two different stages occurring at the same time.

It is not peculiar to persons that their identity over time involves there being relationships of causal or counterfactual dependence between successive stages. The same is true of continuants generally. It is, I think, a point in favour of the psychological continuity account of personal identity that it can

[18]A psychological continuity account is given in Quinton 1962.

be seen as applying to the special case of personal identity an account of identity through time—call it the 'causal continuity account'—which holds of continuants generally.[19]

But the psychological continuity account as so far presented is extremely sketchy. Very little has been said about what constitutes the 'appropriate' causal connections between mental states involved in such continuity. I think that the best way of getting additional light on this is to draw on other parts of the philosophy of mind. What I propose to do now is to consider a widely held (and widely disputed) theory about the nature of mental states, a theory that has been held on grounds having nothing to do with personal identity, and to see what that theory implies about the nature of personal identity. What it implies seems to me a version of the psychological continuity view, and one that puts the notion of an 'appropriate causal connection' in a new and interesting light.

[19]See Shoemaker 1979.

6 Functionalism and Personal Identity

This account of mind is what has come to be called 'functionalism'. What the various versions of it hold in common is that every mental state is a 'functional state', i.e., a state which is definable in terms of its relations (primarily its causal relations) to sensory inputs, behavioural outputs, and (especially) other functional states. A mental state is individuated, and constituted as being the particular mental state it is, by its place in a complex causal network of states. Take, for example, the belief that it is raining. It is characteristic of this state that it is apt to be brought about by certain sense-experiences (but only if the person has certain background beliefs), that in combination with certain other beliefs (e.g., the belief that umbrellas keep off rain) and certain desires (e.g., the desire to keep dry) it leads to certain behaviour (e.g., taking an umbrella if one goes out), and that in combination with certain other beliefs (e.g., the belief that if it is raining then the streets are wet) it leads to still other beliefs (e.g., the belief that the streets are wet). On the functional view, if this characterization were suitably expanded and refined, then no state would count as the belief that it is raining unless it satisfied this characterization, and any state that satisfied it would automatically count as that belief (or, as it is sometimes put, as a 'realization' of that belief). To believe that it is raining, on this view, just *is* to have a state which can be caused to exist in these ways, and which has these sorts of effects when combined with such-and-such other states. And every mental state will have such a functional characterization —one such that a state is a realization of that mental state just in case it satisfies that characterization.[20]

I can indicate only very briefly the considerations that have recommended this view to those who have held it. First, it is compatible with materialism without entailing it. Since the functional characterization of a mental state describes it solely in terms of its causal relations to other states, it leaves open what the 'intrinsic' nature of such a state is. It may be (and this is what most functionalists believe) that what stand in these

[20]See Putnam 1975, and Lewis 1966 and 1972.

networks of causal relations—what 'play these functional roles'—are neurophysiological states of the brain. In that case the states are realized physically; and if all such states are realized physically, materialism is true. But it is also compatible with the functional characterizations that the states should be realized non-physically; thus a mind–body dualist can agree with the functional characterizations without being committed to materialism. The issue of whether materialism or dualism is true is, on this view, an empirical one. This allows the materialist to concede the intelligibility of the dualist view, and even the logical possibility of its being true, while maintaining that it is in fact false.

Second, and closely related to this, functionalism is compatible with, and provides a way of reconciling materialism with, the widely held view that creatures can share the same mental states while differing radically in their internal physical make-ups. The 'abstractness' of functional characterizations allows the same functional state to be realized in a variety of different ways, and if mental states are functional states there is no a priori reason why the same mental state cannot be realized in very different physical states in creatures of different species (humans and dolphins, or, more radically, humans and Martians). In computer jargon, the same 'software' (the same programme) can be realized in different 'hardware'.

Finally, functionalism helps with the problem of other minds. Because it individuates states by their causal, or explanatory, roles, it makes it intelligible that we can know of such states in other persons, as we seem to do, by 'inferences to the best explanation' based on behaviour.

Now let us return to the topic of personal identity. What the functionalist view claims is that it is of the essence of a mental state to be caused in certain ways, and to produce, in conjunction with other mental states, certain effects (behaviour or other mental states). But of course, it is in conjunction with other mental states *of the same person* that a mental state produces the effects it does; and its immediate effects, those the having of which is definitive of its being the mental state it is, will be states (or behaviour) on the part of the *very same person* who had the mental state in question. Thus there is, on the functionalist view, a very intimate connection between the question 'What is the nature of the various mental states?' and the question 'How must different mental states be causally connected in order to be "copersonal", i.e., to belong to one and the same person?'[21]

Unlike the psychological continuity view characterized earlier, the functionalist account of mind has implications concerning the synchronic unity of minds. It is only when the belief that it is raining and the desire to keep dry are copersonal that they tend (in conjunction with other mental states) to lead to such effects as the taking of an umbrella; if the belief is mine and the desire is yours, they will not directly produce any joint effects. And it seems that if a belief and desire do produce (in conjunction with other mental states) just those effects which the functional characterizations of them say they ought to produce if copersonal, then in virtue of this they are copersonal. We can make sense of the idea that a single body might be simultaneously 'animated' by two different minds or consciousnesses; the phenomena that would make it reasonable to believe that this had happened would be similar to, but more extreme than, the phenomena observed in 'split-brain' patients that have led some investigators to think that splitting the brain results in splitting the mind. Whether different mental states that are realized in such a body should count as belonging to the same person, or mind, would seem to turn precisely on whether they are so related that they will jointly have the functionally appropriate sorts of effects.

But one cannot formulate these conditions for synchronic unity of mental states without invoking the notion of diachronic unity. Mental states are synchronically unified in virtue of what they jointly cause or are capable of causing, and what they cause will be something later in time with which they are diachronically unified. Although the effects will include behaviour, I shall focus here on the role of mental states in producing other mental states.

Most functional accounts make it central to the functional nature of mental states that they tend to bring about effects which they, in conjunction with other mental states of the same person, 'rationalize', i.e., make it rational for the person to do (in the case of behaviour) or have (in the case of mental states). A clear case of

[21]See Shoemaker 1979, and Kitcher 1982.

this is that in which a person's beliefs lead, through reasoning, to other beliefs which they entail or otherwise support, or in which beliefs and desires give rise, through deliberation, to a decision which they make reasonable. But we have an instance of it even in what can naturally be regarded as the mere retention of a mental state. I form the intention to do something tomorrow, and when tomorrow comes I do it, from that intention. But while there is a sense in which I retained the same intention throughout, there is also a sense in which the content of my intention was constantly changing; it began as the intention to do something twenty-four hours hence, evolved into the intention to do it twenty-three hours hence, and eventually became the intention to do it *now*. And of course the nature of this change was determined in part by my other mental states, in particular my belief at each point about how much time had passed since the initial formation of the intention. The same thing happens with expectations and with memories.

Instead of speaking of mental states 'evolving into' states having somewhat different contents, let us speak of them as giving rise to 'successor states' having these contents. While the content of a person's mental state (belief, intention, etc.) will to a certain extent depend on the nature of all of his states at earlier times, there will often be a particular state at an earlier time on whose content its content especially depends—and it is of that state that we will call it the 'successor state'. (In some cases, including beliefs expressed by what Quine calls 'eternal sentences', the successor states will have the very same content as their predecessor states; the successor states of my belief that there is no highest prime number will be other tokens of the belief that there is no highest prime number.) On the functionalist view, a mental state is defined in part in terms of what successor states it is liable to give rise to in combination with various other states.

Viewed in this light, what I earlier called 'psychological continuity' is just the playing out over time of the functional natures of the mental states characteristic of persons. To the extent that it consists in psychological similarity between different person-stages, this is due to the fact that in many cases what is required as the successor state of a mental state is just another token of the same state. To the extent that it consists in 'memory-continuity', this is because it belongs to the nature of certain states (sense experiences and intentional actions) that they give rise to successor states of the sort I have called memories from the inside, and because it belongs to the nature of these to perpetuate themselves, i.e., to produce successor states having the same or closely related contents. But psychological continuity is constituted no more by these than it is by the evolution and execution of plans of action, by deliberation and reasoning, and by countless other mental processes. (It should be observed that the 'states' here need not be conscious; most of them will exist in the way my beliefs about Argentina exist when I am giving no thought to Argentina, or in the way my memories of my schooldays exist when I am sound asleep. Also, included under 'states' here are psychological capacities of all kinds; so psychological continuity as here understood will occur even in the case of a newborn infant, although there it will be mainly a matter of retaining psychological capacities that have not yet begun to be exercised.)

Let me return to the point that the functional natures of mental states determine not only the conditions for their diachronic unity but also the conditions for their synchronic unity. It is a commonplace that our minds are sometimes 'compartmentalized'; that they contain subsystems of beliefs, desires and values which are internally coherent but do not cohere well with one another. Thus, for example, there is the man who lives by one set of moral precepts in his private life and quite another in his business dealings, and is unable to see the discrepancy. In such a case the determinants of a person's actions on any given occasion will normally be beliefs and desires belonging to the same 'compartment'; mental states from different compartments either do not combine to influence action at all, or, if they do, result in behaviour which seems incoherent or irrational. The opposite of compartmentalization is 'integration'; a mind is integrated to the extent that the different mental states in it form a consistent set of beliefs and a coherent set of values, and, what goes with this, that what the person does can be seen as rational in the light of all of his beliefs and values, rather than only in the light of some subset of them. As a rough approximation, the unity relation holds between mental states just in case there is at least the possibility of their being integrated into a single set. If the states of what we initially suppose to be one mind were compartmentalized to the extent that it was impossible that states from different compartments should jointly produce effects which they jointly rationalized, then we might speak of there being two 'consciousnesses' there, or perhaps of there being two minds or even two persons, even if the states were all realized in a single human body. There are of course actual cases, cases of 'multiple personality', that approximate to this condition. If we resist saying that there are really two minds or two persons in such cases, this is not (I think) because we are wedded to the principle 'one body, one person'; it is because in the cases that actually occur the compartmentalization is not complete (e.g., one of the personalities will sometimes have memories 'from the inside' of the deeds of the other), and because we think that there is the possibility of integration being at least partially restored.

7 Circularity Circumvented

It may appear that adopting a functionalist account of mental states, far from providing a way of refining the psychological continuity account of personal identity, merely serves to guarantee that such an account will be circular. It seems essential to functional definition that it makes use of the notion of personal identity in defining particular mental states; for what the functional definition of a state tells us is that something counts as a realization of that state if it is such that when combined with such-and-such other states of *the same person* it produces certain effects in *that same person*. If this is how the various mental states are *defined*, it would seem that any reference to mental states implicitly invokes the notion of personal identity, and thus that any attempt to define personal identity in terms of causal relations between mental states will be circular. One cannot, it seems, *both* define mental states in terms of (among other things) personal identity, *and* define personal identity in terms of relations between mental states.

One possible response to this is to admit that the circularity is unavoidable, and to modify one's aims accordingly. This would mean abandoning the claim that one can give a definition, or at any rate a *reductive* definition, of personal identity in terms of psychological continuity. One could still claim, compatibly with this, that the psychological continuity account tells us something important about what personal identity consists in; what it says about the necessary and sufficient conditions of personal identity could be true and non-trivial without amounting to a reductive analysis.[22]

However, I do not think that such a retreat is necessary. For a technique which functionalists have used to avoid another sort of circularity can be applied to this one as well. The belief that it is raining is defined (according to the functionalist) as the state which (among other things) leads to the taking of an umbrella when combined with (among other things) the desire to keep dry; and the desire to keep dry is defined as the state which (among other things) leads to the taking of an umbrella when

[22]This is essentially the line I took in Shoemaker 1979.

combined with (among other things) the belief that it is raining. If we give both definitions we seem to go in a circle—and such circularity seems to be built in to the project of defining mental states in terms of their relations to (among other things) other mental states. The way out, proposed by David Lewis, is to make use of the notion of a 'Ramsey sentence'.[23]

For our present purposes the notion of a Ramsey sentence, and Lewis's employment of it, is best explained by means of an example. Imagine someone whose beliefs about electric charge are summed up in the following sentence: 'Things with positive charge attract things with negative charge and repel things with positive charge; things with negative charge attract things with positive charge and repel things with negative charge; and negative charge can be induced in a rubber comb by rubbing it against wool'. And suppose he is asked to define 'positive charge' and 'negative charge' in terms of this set of beliefs. It might seem that there is no way he could do this without circularity, since each sort of charge is characterized in terms of its relation to the other. However, he could do it as follows. First he constructs the Ramsey sentence of the sentence that expresses his beliefs. This reads 'For some properties F and G, things with F attract things with G and repel things with F; things with G attract things with F and repel things with G; and G can be induced in a rubber comb by rubbing it against wool'. This is obtained by replacing the terms 'negative charge' and 'positive charge' in the original sentence with 'variables' (the letters 'F' and 'G'), thus turning it into an 'open sentence', and then prefacing the open sentence with existential quantifiers (the phrase 'For some properties F and G') binding these variables. The Ramsey sentence does not mention the properties of negative and positive charge by name; it merely says that there exist properties which are related to one another and to certain other phenomena in the way the original sentence said that positive and negative charge are. In terms of this we can define 'positive charge' as follows: x has positive charge $=_{df.}$ for some properties F and G, things with F attract things with G . . . [and so on, as above] . . . and x has F. The term 'negative charge' can be similarly defined. And one can give both definitions without running into circularity, since the

[23]See Lewis 1972.

terms being defined do not occur in the *definiens* of either definition.

To apply this procedure to the task of functionally defining mental states, we begin with a psychological theory containing whatever propositions about the mental states we regard as entering into their functional specification. We then form the Ramsey sentence of the theory (or, on Lewis's version of the procedure, the 'modified Ramsey sentence' which says that there is a unique sequence of states or properties satisfying the open sentence) and extract the functional definitions from it in the way indicated. Now if the only terms that are replaced by variables in forming the Ramsey sentence are mental predicates, then the Ramsey sentence will implicitly invoke the notion of personal identity, for it will speak of states being instantiated in the same person, and of their producing effects in the person in whom they are instantiated. But we can get rid of reference to personal identity in the same way as we got rid of reference to particular mental states. First, let us suppose our psychological theory rewritten in such a way that all talk of personal identity is expressed in terms of the relational predicate 'is copersonal with'. Then in forming the Ramsey sentence we can remove all occurrences of this predicate, just as we remove all occurrences of the mental predicates we want to define; it will be replaced by the relational variable 'stands in R to', which will be bound by an additional existential quantifier ('for some relation R', or, for short, '$\exists R$') at the beginning of the Ramsey sentence. Letting '$\exists R, F, G \ldots (\ldots)$' represent our Ramsey sentence, we can define 'x is copersonal with y' as meaning '$\exists R, F, G \ldots (\ldots \& xRy)$'. Once the notion of copersonality is at hand, we can use it in obvious ways to state the truth conditions for statements of personal identity.

It may be, however, that the relation we define by this procedure is not quite the relation of copersonality. For remember again the case of fission. Suppose that Jones undergoes fission, and that the offshoots are Jones I and Jones II. I ruled earlier that neither Jones I nor Jones II can be identical to the original Jones. If so, the mental states of neither can be copersonal with those of Jones. Yet these states should be 'psychologically continuous' with those of Jones, and this means that they flow from them in the ways prescribed by their functional natures, which means that they should stand to them in the diachronic version of the unity relation defined in terms of our Ramsey sentence. So let us simply dub this relation 'psychological unity'. Synchronic psychological unity will always be copersonality. And diachronic psychological unity will be copersonality as long as no 'branching' (e.g., fission) has occurred in the development of the succession of states.

It is not at all my purpose here to defend the view that persons are logical constructions, *à la* Russell, out of person-stages, mental states, or momentary experiences. To me it is quite obvious that the conceptually prior notion is that of a person, not that of a momentary person-stage or experience. And my view is just the opposite of the conventionalist view often held by those who propose that we can define persons as sums or series of person-stages (or momentary mental states) that are related in certain ways. For part of my point is that the nature of personal identity is, in effect, determined by the nature of the various sorts of mental states persons have. Once we have said what the mental states are, and specified their functional natures, there is no room for conventional decision about what the identity conditions of their subjects are—those identity conditions are built in to the nature of the states.

Here I have done no more than hint at how functional definitions of mental states would go; and no functionalist has offered more than a sketch of a functional definition of any mental state. We are a long way from having a full account of the nature of mental states. And if I am right, we are equally far from having a full account of personal identity; for a full account of either would amount to a full account of the other.

8 Unity of Consciousness and Self-Consciousness

The phrase 'unity of consciousness' is ambiguous; it can refer either to the unity (copersonality) of conscious states, or to the consciousness of this unity, i.e., the consciousness of a variety (or 'manifold') of mental states *as* unified into a single consciousness, namely one's own. A plausible view, associated with Kant, is that unity of consciousness in the first sense in some way involves unity of consciousness in the second, i.e., involves self-consciousness. This fits with the functional account of mind, and the psychological continuity account of personal identity, I have been sketching.

I have suggested that the unity of mental states involves integration or at least the possibility of integration, where the integration of mental states involves their producing effects which they jointly rationalize, and requires a substantial degree of internal coherence. And integration seems to involve self-consciousness. For a system of mental states to remain integrated over a period of time, its contents must be constantly changing in the light of new experience. Often this will require reasoning and empirical testing aimed at discovering how conflicts between beliefs, or between desires, should be resolved; and in order to know what reasoning is called for, and what tests to conduct, the person must know what his competing beliefs and desires are. Assuming that the existence of beliefs and desires requires the possibility of their being integrated into a larger system, and that such integration depends on self-consciousness, it would appear that the capacity for being conscious of such states in oneself is inseparable from the capacity for having them.

As noted in section 1, the nature of our self-knowledge, both our awareness of our currently mental states and our memory knowledge of our own identity, is one of the sources of philosophical perplexity about the nature of persons. When one is introspectively aware of one's thoughts, feelings, beliefs and desires, one is not presented to oneself as a flesh and blood person, and one does not seem to be presented to oneself as an *object* at all. This comes out in the fact, noted by Wittgenstein in the *Blue Book*, that the use of 'I' in first-person experience ascriptions does not involve the recognition, or identification, of a person; when I say 'I have an itch', or 'I think so-and-so', it is not the case that I know this because I observe (by 'inner sense') *somebody* having an itch, and identify that person as myself.[24] For identification goes with the possibility of mis-identification, and it is impossible that I should know intro-spectively that someone has an itch and mistakenly take that person to be me. Likewise, when I know on the basis of memory that I did so-and-so in the past, it is not the case that I remember someone doing that thing and identify that person as myself by what I remember about him. I do not make such an identification on the basis of bodily criteria, but I do not make it on the basis of non-bodily criteria either.[25] It is essential to remembering one's past actions and experiences 'from the inside' that one's past self, the subject of those actions and experiences, does not enter into the content of one's memory in the way other persons do.

If one is struck by the fact that one is not presented to onself in introspection as a *bodily* object, this may seem to be a reason for accepting a dualist position like Descartes's, according to which the self is a non-material substance. If one goes on to notice that one is not presented to oneself in introspection as an object *at all*, this may seem to support the view of David Hume that the self is only a 'bundle of perceptions'—that there is not, over and above one's individual thoughts, feelings, and so on, a subject or substance (material or non- material) that 'has' them.[26] Again, if one is struck by the fact that one uses no *bodily* criteria of identity in making first-person memory claims like 'I played tennis yesterday', this may seem to support the view (which we have found independent reasons for believing) that the criteria of personal identity are non-bodily. If one goes on to notice that one does not seem to use *any* criteria of identity in making such claims, this may seem to support the quite different view, held by Bishop Butler and Thomas Reid, that there are no constitutive criteria of personal identity at all—that personal identity is 'indefinable' and does not *consist* in anything.

[24]See Wittgenstein, *Blue and Brown Books*, p. 66. See also Shoemaker 1968.
[25]See Shoemaker 1963, ch. 4.
[26]Hume, *Enquiry*, p. 252.

But a little reflection shows that the facts about self-knowledge are entirely compatible with the functionalist psychological continuity view I have been sketching—and that view, as we will see more fully in the next section, is entirely compatible with a materialist view of the world.

In discussing the nature of self-knowledge we should distinguish two questions: (1) What makes a belief a belief about oneself? (2) What is distinctive about the way in which we come to have such beliefs in the cases in which they constitute introspective self-knowledge? In discussing (1) I will interpret 'about oneself' in such a way that if one is, say, the tallest man in the room, but does not realize this, then one's belief that the tallest man in the room plays golf will not count as a belief about oneself. Beliefs about oneself are the sorts of beliefs one expresses with the use of the first-person pronouns. A great deal could be said about such beliefs. But I believe that the most important thing about them, conceptually speaking, is the distinctive role they play in the determination of action (which here includes the mental activity involved in deliberation and reasoning, as well as bodily action). If I am the long lost son of X, learning that the long lost son of X can collect a fortune by presenting himself in Cleveland will not send me towards Cleveland unless I know, or believe, that I am the long lost son of X.[27] It is in terms of this distinctive role that a functionalist should answer question (1).

The brief answer to (2) is that we are so constituted that our being in certain states directly produces in us beliefs about ourselves to the effect that we are in those states, and that such beliefs count as knowledge because they are reliably produced. I have suggested that it is of the essence of certain mental states that they produce such self-knowledge. What distinguishes this from other cases in which the fact that so-and-so produces knowledge that so-and-so is the directness of the connection. It is not mediated by the production of other beliefs from which the final belief is inferred (in the way a historical event produces a belief in its existence by producing present evidence of its existence), and it is not mediated by anything analogous to a sense-impression. The latter point is especially important; it shows that the knowledge in question is radically different from

[27]See Perry 1977 and 1979.

perceptual knowledge. The reason one is not presented to oneself 'as an object' in self-awareness is that self-awareness is not perceptual awareness, i.e., is not the sort of awareness in which objects are presented. It is awareness of facts unmediated by awareness of objects. But it is worth noting that if one were aware of oneself as an object in such cases (as one is in fact aware of oneself as an object when one sees oneself in a mirror), this would not help to explain one's self-knowledge. For awareness that the presented object was φ would not tell one that one was oneself φ, unless one had identified the object as oneself; and one could not do this unless one already had some self-knowledge, namely the knowledge that one is the unique possessor of whatever set of properties of the presented object one took to show it to be oneself. Perceptual self-knowledge presupposes non-perceptual self-knowledge, so not all self-knowledge can be perceptual.[28] Recognition of these facts should help to dispel the notion that the nature of self-knowledge supports the Cartesian view that the self is a peculiar sort of object, or the Humean view that it is no sort of object at all.

A special case of self-knowledge being directly produced by the fact known is that in which one knows that one remembers 'from the inside' a past action or experience. Here one's self enters into the content of what is directly known, not as the subject of the past action or experience (although in fact it will be that), but as the subject of the present remembering. But since in fact the only actions or experiences anyone ever remembers from the inside are his own (i.e., since in fact 'fission' does not occur), it is a short step from the knowledge that one remembers a past action or experience from the inside to the knowledge that it was oneself that did the action or had the experience. Indeed, it is such a short step that only a philosopher would notice that it is a step at all. It is the shortness of this step, plus the directness of one's knowledge of what one remembers, that constitutes the special access people have in memory to facts about their own identity.

[28]See Shoemaker 1968, pp. 560–4.

9 Mind and Body

Any view of personal identity which allows for the possibility of a person changing bodies, as in Locke's prince–cobbler case or my Brown–Brownson case, is incompatible with the view that a person is simply identical to his body. For if a person is capable of undergoing a change of body, he has a property—the 'modal' property of being able to exist at a time or place at which that body does not exist—which his body does not have, and so (by Leibniz's Law) cannot be identical to it.

But this conclusion, that the person is not identical to his body, gives no support to dualism, and is in fact perfectly compatible with a materialist view of the world. Here an analogy with another part of the philosophy of mind may be instructive. Some materialistically inclined philosophers have maintained that sensations and other mental states are identical to brain processes—e.g., that pain might be identical with the firing of C-fibres. One ground that has been given for rejecting this view is that even if pain is invariably correlated with C-fibre firing in human beings, it seems entirely possible that in some other species it is not so correlated—and if this is a possibility, pain has a modal property (being able to occur without C-fibre firing occurring) which C-fibre firing does not have, and so cannot be identical to it. A functionalist account of mind allows this rejection of the 'psychophysical identity theory' to be reconciled with materialism. According to it, pain is a functional property which can be realized in one way in us (perhaps in C-fibre firing) and in some quite different way in the Martians. All that materialism requires is that all of the actual realizations of mental states be physical; it is compatible with their being different in different species or different creatures. Analogously, one might say, while the way personal identity is realized in us involves (at least normally) the identity of the body, there are other possible ways in which it could be realized. The one alternative way we have considered so far involved the transfer of the brain, and might be said to depend on the fact that in us it is in the first instance in the identity of the brain that personal identity is realized. It seems obvious that this way of realizing personal identity is compatible with materialism. And the same is true of other ways I shall consider.

If the account sketched in sections 6 and 7 is correct, the analogy here is a very close one. I suggested there that the relation of 'copersonality', or 'psychological unity', might itself be defined functionally. Given the intimate internal connections there are between the notions of the particular mental states and the notion of copersonality, it is impossible for the mental states to be realized physically without the relation of copersonality also being realized physically. For the realization of a mental state involves the existence of a mechanism whereby it stands in the causal connections that are definitive of it—i.e., a mechanism whereby it produces copersonal successor states in conjunction with copersonal states simultaneous with it. If this mechanism is entirely physical, so will be the realization of the relationship of copersonality.

In section 8 I argued that the facts about the nature of our self-knowledge provide no sound basis for a dualist (anti-materialist) view of mind and personal identity. Given this, given what science tells us about the world, and given that (as the functionalist account implies) there is no a priori reason why mental states cannot be realized physically, then in the absence of compelling empirical evidence that mental states are realized non-physically we ought to believe that they are realized physically.

10 The Brain-State Transfer Device

A few paragraphs back I spoke of the physical realization of mental states as requiring a 'mechanism'. It might be supposed that the physical realization of a mechanism would have to be a physical body of some sort. And then it might seem implicit in what I have said that if materialism is true personal identity must always be realized in the identity of some sort of physical body— if not in the identity of something like a complete human body, then at least in the identity of a brain or of some organ that plays the sort of functional role the brain plays in us.[29] In order to consider whether this is so, and also in order to consider some of the objections that have been raised against accounts of personal identity like that presented here, I have to consider yet another hypothetical example.

A number of philosophers have envisaged the possibility of a device which records the state of one brain and imposes that state on a second brain by restructuring it so that it has exactly the state the first brain had at the beginning of the operation.[30] We will suppose that this process obliterates the first brain, or at any rate obliterates its current state. Discussions of this example usually proceed on the assumption that mental states are at least 'supervenient' on brain states, which means that creatures cannot differ in their mental states without differing in their brain states, and therefore that the 'recipient' of a total brain-state transfer would have exactly the same mental states the 'donor' had immediately before. Philosophers who have discussed this sort of case have differed in their intuitions as to whether the brain-state transfer would amount to a person's changing bodies—whether, as I shall put it, the procedure would be 'person-preserving'. Some think it would. Others think that it would amount to killing the original person and at the same time creating (or converting someone into) a psychological duplicate of him.

Initially, I think, most people are inclined to take the latter view. But one can tell a story which enhances the plausibility of the former view. Imagine a society living in an environment in

---

[29]See Wiggins 1967, p. 51.
[30]See Williams 1970, p. 162, and Nozick 1981, p. 39.

which an increase in some sort of radiation has made it impossible for a human body to remain healthy for more than a few years. Being highly advanced technologically, the society has developed the following procedure for dealing with this. For each person there is a stock of duplicate bodies, cloned from cells taken from that person and grown by an accelerated process in a radiation-proof vault, where they are then stored. Periodically a person goes into the hospital for a 'body-change'. This consists in his total brain-state being transferred to the brain of one of his duplicate bodies. At the end of the procedure the original body is incinerated. We are to imagine that in this society going in for a body-change is as routine an occurrence as going to have one's teeth cleaned is in ours. It is taken for granted by everyone that the procedure is person-preserving. One frequently hears remarks like 'I can't meet you for lunch on Tuesday, because that is the day for my body-change; let's make it Wednesday instead'. All of the social practices of the society presuppose that the procedure is person-preserving. The brain-state recipient is regarded as owning the property of the brain-state donor, as being married to the donor's spouse, and as holding whatever offices, responsibilities, rights, obligations, etc. the brain-state donor held. If it is found that the brain-state donor had committed a crime, everyone regards it as just that the brain-state recipient should be punished for it.

Let us suppose, for now, that materialism is true; the world does not contain any non-material substances, and all of the entities in it are composed exclusively of the entities recognized by physics. The members of my hypothetical society know this, and they know precisely what happens, physically speaking, in the brain-state transfer procedure (for short, the BST-procedure). There is no clear sense in which they can be said to be mistaken about a matter of fact in regarding the procedure as person-preserving. If we confronted such a society, there would, I think, be a very strong case for saying that what *they* mean by 'person' is such that the BST-procedure *is* person-preserving (using 'person' in *their* sense). And, what goes with this, it would be very hard to maintain that they are being irrational when, being under no misconception concerning matters of fact, they willingly submit themselves to the BST-procedure. But there would also be a strong reason for saying that what they mean by 'person' is what we mean by it; they call the same things persons, offer the same sorts of characterizations of what sorts of things persons are, and attach the same kinds of social consequences to judgements of personal identity—i.e., personal identity has with them the same connections with moral responsibility, ownership of property, etc. as it does with us. But if they are right in thinking that the BST-procedure is person-preserving, and if they mean the same by 'person' as we do, then it seems that *we* ought to regard the BST-procedure as person-preserving.

A variety of objections have been raised against the view that anything like the BST-procedure could be person-preserving, and some of these would also apply, if valid, to the view that the brain-transplant procedure (as in the Brown–Brownson case) could be person-preserving. Some of these will be discussed in the following sections. Here I want to consider the bearing of this example on the question of whether a materialist view of mind requires personal identity to be realized in the identity of some sort of physical body.

On the face of it, if one allows that the BST-procedure is person-preserving, one must hold that the answer to this question is 'no'. For the BST-procedure does not involve the transfer of any bodily organ, or of any matter at all, from the one body to the other. All that is transferred, it is natural to say, is 'information'. If we have personal identity here, it is apparently not carried by the identity of any body. Yet it seems clear that one is not committed to dualism, or the rejection of materialism, in holding that the procedure is person-preserving; on the contrary, the plausibility of holding the latter seems to depend on the materialist assumption that mental states are realized in, or at least supervenient on, states of the brain.

But how can this be reconciled with my claim in section 9 that the physical realization of a mental state requires the existence of a physical 'mechanism' whereby it stands, or is capable of standing, in the functionally appropriate causal relations to other mental states of the same person, including its successor states? I think that what one must say, if one allows that the BST-procedure would be person-preserving, is that in the circumstances I have imagined the mechanism in which the mental states of a person are realized does not include just the person's body or brain; it also includes the BST-device, and perhaps the social institutions that govern its use. For it is in virtue of the existence of all this that mental states existing immediately before a body-change produce the functionally appropriate successor states. What one has here is a non-standard (relative to us) way of realizing mental states and the relation of copersonality, one that relies for the most part on the mechanism in which these are realized in us, but which supplements these with an additional mechanism. The mechanism as a whole does not consist in any *single* physical body, or even depend on any single one (for the BST-device could wear out and be replaced several times during a person's lifetime). Thus it is that we have personal identity without the identity of any body, even though nothing non-physical is involved.

11 Personal Identity and Animal Identity

If we take the term 'human beings' to refer to a certain species of animals, namely *homo sapiens*, it does not appear to be any sort of necessary truth that all persons are human beings. Maybe Locke was right in thinking that a highly intelligent parrot could count as a person.[31] Maybe porpoises could turn out to be persons. Maybe there are creatures elsewhere in the universe ('Martians'), biologically unrelated to us, who ought to count as persons. But it hardly seems controversial that we ourselves, and all of the creatures we ordinarily call persons, are human beings. And in being human beings we are animals of a certain kind.

But this poses a difficulty for the claim that anything like the BST-procedure could be person-preserving. If a person *is* an animal, then, it would seem, whenever we have that person we have that animal, and whenever we have that animal we have that person. But suppose that by the BST-procedure the brain states of body A are transferred to the brain of body B. It is proposed that we say in this case that the person who formerly had body A now has body B. But can we plausibly say that the person with body B after the transfer is the same *animal* as the person who formerly had body A? It would seem not. But if it is not the same animal, then, it would seem, it also cannot be the same person. This difficulty also arises, although perhaps not with equal force, for the claim that a brain transfer like that envisaged in the Brown–Brownson case could be person-preserving; if asked whether Brownson is the same animal as Brown, one's initial inclination (I think) would be to say 'no'.

John Locke's response to this difficulty was to distinguish between the identity of a *person* and the identity of a *man*, and to hold that the latter does, while the former does not, involve the identity of an animal (which in turn requires retaining the same living human body). He thought that in his prince–cobbler case the man with the cobbler's body after the soul-transfer would be the same person, but not the same man, as the prince. This hardly conforms to the normal usage of the term

[31]See Locke, *Essay*, pp. 333–4.

'man'; I think that most of us would be prepared to say that we have the same person in this case only if we were also prepared to say that we have the same man. But the crucial question is whether any sense can be made of Locke's view that something which is a human being can be the same person as someone in the past without being the same human being or the same animal.

One way of trying to make sense of this would be to adopt P. T. Geach's view that identity is relative.[32] On this view, every identity judgement should be regarded as being of the form 'x is the same F as y', where 'F' is a 'sortal term' (like 'man', or 'tree', or 'automobile'), and it is possible for x to be the same F as y and not the same G as y, even though x and y are both F's and G's. On such a view, it is possible for Brownson to be the same person as Brown but not the same animal (human being), even though Brownson and Brown are both animals (human beings) as well as persons. However, this way out is not available to me, since I find the theory of identity as relative unacceptable.[33]

The only other way of making sense of the Lockean view is to maintain that what is (predicatively) a person is not (predicatively) an animal or a human being. In taking this view one can allow that there is a sense of 'is' in which a person is an animal. But this will not be the 'is' of predication or of identity; it will be, perhaps, the sort of 'is' we have in 'The statue is a hunk of bronze'—it will mean something like 'is composed of the very same stuff as'. Arguably, the statue and the hunk of bronze are not one and the same thing, since if the hunk of bronze were hammered into another statue, the statue we had originally would no longer exist, but the hunk of bronze would still be there. So two things, the statue and the hunk of bronze, can occupy the same place and share the same matter and the same non-historical properties.[34] And whatever we say of the hunk of bronze, the statue does share its space with one entity that is incontestably non-identical with it, namely the quantity of bronze of which it is composed.[35] The suggestion is that a person 'is' an animal, not in the sense of being identical to one, but in the sense of sharing its matter with one.[36] One could also

[32]See Geach 1967.
[33]See Perry 1970, and Wiggins 1967 and 1980.
[34]See Wiggins 1967, and Shoemaker 1970b.
[35]For the notion of a quantity, see Cartwright 1970.
[36]Here I am indebted to Alan Sidelle.

say that the animal is that in which the person is physically realized at a given time. On such a view it is possible for a person to 'be' one animal (human being) at one time and another animal (human being) at another time.

I think that there is no doubt that this view is prima facie counterintuitive. One's initial inclination, certainly, is to say that one is an animal and a human being in just the sense in which one is a person. But the alternatives to this view, call it (A), seem to be the following three views: (B) identity is relative, (C) it is logically impossible for a person to change bodies, and (D) while there are logically possible cases in which a person changes bodies, these are also cases in which an animal changes bodies. It seems to me that (A) is clearly preferable to (B) and (C). And it is hardly more counterintuitive than (D). Here the best we can do is to accept the least objectionable of several counterintuitive views. I am not sure whether this is (A) or (D), and shall not attempt to choose between them.

12 The Duplication Objection

A common objection to the view that something like the BST-procedure could be person-preserving goes along the following lines. It might happen that the BST-device misfunctions, and produces the states of brain A in brain B without obliterating those states in brain A, or produces these states not only in brain B but also in brain C. If this happened the post-transfer possessor of brain B could not be identical to the pre-transfer possessor of brain A—or at any rate, he could not be so simply in virtue of his psychological continuity with that person. But surely (it is said), whether a person X at time t_2 is identical to person Y existing at an earlier time t_1 cannot depend on whether there happens to be another person Z whose state at t_2 is related to Y's state at t_1 in the same way that X's state at t_2 is related to it. So even if the machine functions properly, and there is no duplication, the post-transfer possessor of brain B cannot be identical to the pre-transfer possessor of brain A in virtue of his psychological continuity with him.[37]

One could meet this objection just by stipulating that the BST-procedure is such as to make such duplication nomologically impossible—it essentially depends on the states of the original brain being obliterated, and is such that the states can be transferred to only one brain. But I shall not rely on such a stipulation. Let us suppose that duplication of the sort envisaged is nomologically possible, and that only the vigilance of the operators of the BST-device prevents it from happening.

The duplication objection cannot be that the psychological continuity account of personal identity (which is presupposed by the view that the BST-procedure is person-preserving) has the absurd consequence that both post-transfer duplicates (the A-brain person and the B-brain person, or the A-brain person and the C-brain person) are identical to the original A-brain person. We guarded the account against that objection by having it say, not that personal identity consists in psychological continuity *simpliciter*, but that it consists in *non-branching*

---

[37]For this general sort of objection, see Williams 1957–58. For a recent formulation, see Wiggins 1980, pp. 95–6.

psychological continuity. The objection is rather that this way of guarding against that absurd consequence makes the identity depend on something it cannot depend on. Later on (in section 16) I will concede something (not much) to the duplication objection. Here I want to reveal the extent to which it rests on confusion.

Suppose that the BST-device functions correctly, and that after the transfer only brain B has the states that brain A had immediately before the transfer. Let 'Smith' name the pre-transfer A-brain person, and let 'George' name the post-transfer B-brain person. It might appear that my version of the psychological continuity account, with its 'non-branching' provision, commits us to saying the following: since there was no branching in the psychologically continuous series of person-stages connecting Smith before the transfer and George after the transfer, George and Smith are the same person; but the BST-device could have misfunctioned and left brain A unaffected, in which case Smith and George would have been different persons. Now this would be an absurd consequence. If Smith and George are in fact one and the same person, they are necessarily the same, and there is no possible circumstance in which they are different persons.[38] But it is a confusion to think that this absurd consequence follows from the non-branching psychological continuity view (together with the assumption that the BST-device in fact functioned correctly, but could have misfunctioned in the way envisaged).

What does follow is this: in fact the post-transfer B-brain person is identical to the pre-transfer A-brain person, but if the BST-device had misfunctioned in the way envisaged, the post-transfer B-brain person would not have been the pre-transfer A-brain person. This does not offend against the principle that identity holds necessarily if at all, and it is analogous to the following observation (which is true on one natural reading of it): in fact the president of the US in 1982 is the only former governor of California who began his career as a movie actor, but if Carter had received a lot more votes then the president of the US in 1982 would not have been that former governor. The crucial difference here is that whereas names like 'George' and

[38]Here I assume the truth of Saul Kripke's view that identity propositions having names as terms are necessarily true if true at all. See Kripke 1980.

'Smith' are what Saul Kripke has called 'rigid designators', and have the same reference in talk about hypothetical or counter-factual situations ('other possible worlds') as they do in talk about the actual situation, definite descriptions like 'the post-transfer B-body person' and 'the president of the US in 1982' are not rigid designators.[39] It is only identity statements whose terms are rigid designators that have to be necessarily true if true at all, and so cannot be such that they are true but might have been false. It is not possible that George should have failed to be Smith; what is possible (on the non-branching psycholog-ical continuity view) is that George (i.e., Smith) should not have been the post-transfer B-brain person, either because he failed to survive the transfer or because he survived it as the post-transfer A-brain person. If either of the latter possibilities had been realized, the post-transfer B-brain person would have been somebody else—perhaps somebody who was created (with a set of memories corresponding to George's past) by the BST-procedure.

In part, I think, the duplication objection is the result of a failure to distinguish rigid and non-rigid designators and their roles in identity statements. But it has other sources as well. One of these, which comes out in a version of the duplication objection raised by Richard Swinburne, is connected with one of the central issues about personal identity.[40]

Recall the 'fission' example of section 4 which involves the transplantation of the two hemispheres of someone's brain into two different bodies. Swinburne envisages a theory of personal identity which holds (as indeed our psychological continuity theory seems to do) that whether the post-operative owner of one hemisphere is identical to the original person depends on whether the transplantation of the other hemisphere 'takes'. One of his objections to this is the one we have already answered. He thinks that such a view has the absurd conse-quence that 'Who I am depends on whether you exist' (1973–74, p. 236). Now there is a perfectly good sense in which 'who I am' *can* depend on whether you exist; e.g., whether I am the heir to someone's fortune may depend on this (if his will stipulates that I inherit only if you no longer exist). What

39See Kripke 1980.
40See Swinburne 1973–74.

cannot depend on whether you exist is whether I am identical to some particular person. But the theory in question does not imply that there could be such a dependence. To be sure, if I am the post-operative possessor of the left brain hemisphere, then in order to establish whether I am identical to the original person I might have to establish whether the transplantation of the right hemisphere was successful. But suppose that it was in fact successful (and the post-operative possessor of the right hemisphere is you). In that case neither of us is identical to the original person. And it would be wrong to say that if the other half-brain transplantation had failed, then I would have been the original person; one should say instead that if it had failed *I* would not exist (although there would exist someone with this body and these memories). If we suppose instead that the actual situation is that in which the other transplant failed, and in which I am identical to the original person (according to our theory), then the true counterfactual is not that if the other transplant had succeeded I would not have been the original person, but that in that case I (= the original person) would no longer exist.

But Swinburne says that the view in question has a second absurd consequence, namely that

> The way for a man to ensure his own survival is to ensure the non-existence of future persons too similar to himself. Suppose the mad surgeon had told P_1 before the operation what he was intending to do . . . P_1 is unable to escape the clutches of the mad surgeon, but is nevertheless very anxious to survive the operation. If the empiricist theory in question is correct there is an obvious policy which will guarantee his survival. He can bribe one of the nurses to ensure that the right half-brain does *not* survive successfully. (1973–74, p. 237)

I think that it can be agreed that it does seem absurd for P_1 to try to guarantee his survival by bribing the nurse. But I think that it is not absurd for the reason Swinbourne thinks it is.

13 Survival and the Importance of Identity

What is at stake here is what it is that we really care about when we care about our own survival and our own future well-being. Swinburne makes the natural assumption that when I want to survive it is essential to the satisfaction of my want that I, the very person who is now wanting this, should exist in the future. But this can be questioned.

Consider another variant of our half-brain transplant case. Suppose that half of my brain and all of the rest of my body are ridden with cancer, and that my only hope for survival is for my healthy half-brain to be transplanted to another body. There are two transplantation procedures available. The first, which is inexpensive and safe (so far as the prospects of the recipient are concerned) involves first transplanting the healthy hemisphere and then destroying (or allowing to die) the diseased hemisphere that remains. The other, which is expensive and risky (the transplant may not take, or it may produce a psychologically damaged person) involves first destroying the diseased hemisphere and then transplanting the other. Which shall I choose? Notice that if I choose the first procedure there will be, for a short while, two persons psychologically continuous with the original person (me), and therefore that on the non-branching psychological continuity theory the recipient of the healthy hemisphere cannot count as me. If I choose the second procedure, on the other hand, then at no point will the recipient (the post-operative possessor of the healthy hemisphere) have any 'competitor' for the status of being me, so it seems that he can count as me (if the transplantation takes). Should I therefore choose the expensive and risky procedure? This seems absurd. The thing to do is to choose the first procedure, even though (I think) it guarantees that the transplant recipient will not be me.

How can this be? Am I relying on some moral principle that requires one to so act as to maximize the number and well-being of future persons, independently of who those persons are, even if this involves sacrificing oneself? No. The reason is that whether the future person will be me is *in a case like this* of no importance to me. This is why I find it absurd for P_1 in Swinburne's example to bribe the nurse with the object of ensuring that the left half-brain recipient is himself; I see that if I were in P_1's position, bribing the nurse would contribute nothing to giving me what I really want in wanting to survive.

Consider again our original fission case, in which both half-brain transplantations take and there are two later persons who are psychologically continuous with the owner of the original brain. How should the original person view the prospect of this? Let us suppose that he accepts the analysis according to which neither offshoot will be him (where 'be him' means 'be identical to him'). Does this mean that he must view the impending fission as his death and replacement by duplicates? Remember that the offshoots will be (and we can suppose him to know that they will be) psychologically continuous with him in all of the ways in which a person at one time is continuous with himself at other times. Not only will they remember his past; they will also be influenced by his intentions and motivated by his desires (or by desires which are 'successor states' of his pre-operative desires). For him now to deliberate about and plan their future careers would be just as efficacious as it is for a person to deliberate about and plan his own future career. Their future sufferings and delights, their prospects of success and failure, could not be a matter of indifference to him. Indeed, if his attitude towards these were not essentially like those a person normally has towards his own future sufferings, delights, successes and failures, then we would not have full psychological continuity between the original person and the offshoots.

Since cases of this sort do not occur, we are ill-equipped with language for talking about them. One way of doing so, adopted by Derek Parfit, is to sever the connection between our current notion of survival and the concept of identity, and to speak of the original person as 'surviving as' both offshoots.[41] The rationale for doing this is that the attitudes that are appropriate in a case in which one believes that one will survive as a person of a certain description (fear of that person's suffering, hope for that person's success, etc.) are ones which a man could appropriately have towards the future states of both of his

[41]See Parfit 1971b.

offshoots in a case of impending fission. But even if one does not want to call this survival, one can allow that it could be just as good (or, as the case might be, just as bad) as survival.

Considerations like these have led some philosophers to maintain that what matters in survival is not identity, *per se*, but the psychological continuity or connectedness which normally accompany and constitute it, namely when there is no branching.[42] This is not, certainly, the view that recommends itself to pre-analytic intuition. One's initial inclination is to say that if one cares especially about the future person who will be psychologically continuous with one, this is because one believes that that person will be oneself. What reflection on the fission case suggests is that it is just the other way around; one cares about the future person who will be oneself because (normally) it is that person who is psychologically continuous with one.[43]

To the extent that our having this concern is a contingent fact about us, the explanation of it no doubt lies in part in evolutionary considerations. But there is something ludicrous about the idea of a competition for survival between creatures having such a concern and otherwise similar creatures who totally lack it. For the latter are, I think, inconceivable. If a creature is enough like us to be capable of pleasure and pain, and to be able to envisage future states of affairs at all, it will have some degree of future directed concern. Special circumstances aside, it is inconceivable that a creature should be indifferent to its *present* pleasures and pains. But the future is continuous with the present; it is inconceivable that a creature should want its present pain to cease, or its present pleasure to continue, and yet be indifferent as to whether it has a qualitatively identical pain or pleasant experience a moment hence. It seems implicit in knowing what pain and pleasure are that (other things being equal, of course) one wants one's immediate future to be free of the one and to contain the other. To a certain extent, then, this special concern for one's own future well-being is built into the nature of human mental states.

[42]See Shoemaker 1970a, and Parfit 1971b. See also Perry 1976a.
[43]Several philosophers have proposed ways—which I have not the space to discuss here—of reconciling the claim that what we care about in survival is identity, with the intuition that if faced with the prospect of fission one would (or reasonably could) care about each offshoot as if it were oneself. See Perry 1972, Lewis 1976, and Nozick 1981, pp. 62–8.

14 Is Personal Identity 'Simple and Unanalysable'?

Bishop Butler and Thomas Reid distinguished between the identity we ascribe to persons and that we ascribe to ships, trees, etc., claiming that the former is identity in the 'strict and philosophical sense', while the latter is identity only in a 'loose and popular sense'. Part of what they had in mind is that personal identity is 'indefinable' or 'unanalysable' in a way the (so-called) identity of these other sorts of things is not. Apparently they would allow that the identity of a ship over time can be analysed as consisting in some sort of relation between successive ship-stages, but only because they think that this is identity only in a 'loose and popular sense', i.e., that unlike the identity of persons, it is not really *identity*.

Let us begin with the claim about indefinability. We can agree that the notion of identity, as such, cannot be defined or analysed beyond specifying the logical features of it mentioned in section 2, and that the latter does not amount to defining it in terms of more primitive notions. Sometimes it is supposed that if one tries to give an account of the identity over time of so-and-so's (persons, trees, ships, etc.), then one is trying to define a *kind* of identity (personal identity, ship identity, or whatever). But I rejected the claim that there are kinds of identity in section 11, when I rejected the relative identity view. If one is analysing any concept in giving an account of personal identity, it is the concept of a person. And the fact that the concept of identity, as such, is relatively unanalysable cannot be used to argue that we cannot analyse the concept of a person by (among other things) specifying the identity conditions for persons. As John Perry has pointed out, if we want to convey to someone the concept of a baseball game, we will want to convey to him (among other things) what marks off one baseball game from another (so that he will not think that different parts of a double-header are parts of a single game, or that different games being played simultaneously on the same field are parts of a single game).[44] What we are doing here is using the notion of identity—the *one* notion of (numerical) identity we have

[44]See Perry, 1975b, pp. 7–9.

(and a notion than which none is stricter)—to explicate a particular concept (that of a baseball game) by giving the identity conditions for things that fall under it. We are doing nothing different when we offer an account of personal identity, such as the psychological continuity account.

One source of the Butler–Reid view was mentioned in section 2; this is the confusion about the notion of substance which leads to the view that in the 'strict and philosophical sense' of 'same', the same thing cannot be composed of different stuff (different 'substance', in one sense of the word) at different times. If combined with a materialist view of persons, and the undoubted fact that persons are constantly changing their material composition, this would lead to the conclusion (which was held by Hume, although he was no materialist) that personal identity is 'fictitious', i.e., not 'strict and philosophical'. But usually those who have held this view have been dualists, and have held that the identity of a person consists in the identity of an immaterial substance and so is not undermined by the fact that the matter that makes up a person's body is replaced bit by bit over time. Why have these philosophers been so sure that it is the same immaterial substance that exists at different times in what a person regards as his own history? No doubt this conviction stems in part from the seeming immediacy of a person's memory knowledge of his own past. The immediate deliverance of memory seems to be 'I did (experienced) so-and-so'; and because this does seem to be an immediate deliverance of memory, rather than something inferred from remembered evidence of identity, it is natural to suppose that in memory one has direct access to personal identity itself.[45] And then, as not uncommonly happens in philosophy, the immediacy of the knowledge is taken as proof of the simplicity of what is known.

But the plausibility of this way of thinking ought to wither when one reflects on a famous footnote in the 'Paralogisms' of Kant's *Critique of Pure Reason*. By analogy with the case in which one elastic ball communicates its motion to another, which in turn communicates it to another, and so on, Kant imagines

---

[45]If fission is a possibility, it is misleading to say that 'I did (experienced) so-and-so' is an 'immediate deliverance of memory'. See the final paragraph of section 8.

a whole series of substances of which the first transmits its state together with its consciousness to the second, the second its own state with that of the preceding substance to the third, and this in turn the state of all the preceding substances together with its own consciousness and with their consciousness to another. The last substance would then be conscious of all the states of the previously changed substances, as being its own states, because they would have been transferred to it together with the consciousness of them. (p. 343)

Supposing that such a succession of substances is possible, nothing in the nature of one's self-consciousness shows that this is not what we have in ordinary cases of what we count as personal identity. Kant concludes this passage by saying 'And yet it would not have been one and the same person in all these states'. Here, I think, Kant is assuming for the sake of discussion the metaphysical conception of a person—the person as a Cartesian substance —which he is out to undermine. This seems to have been Butler's conception. So it would not be far wrong to say that Kant's example shows that Butler's view leads to scepticism about the knowability of personal identity. Obviously, none of our third-person evidence of personal identity tends in the slightest to favour the view that in what we regard as cases of the persistence of a person over time there is a single immaterial substance rather than a Kantian succession of different ones, each communicating its consciousness to the next (or, in the terminology of section 6, the states of each producing their successor states in the next). Kant's point is that the situation is no different when we consider the first-person evidence. The upshot is that on the Butler–Reid view, we have no good evidence at all for believing that persons ever persist over time. And it seems reasonable to take this as a *reductio ad absurdum* of that view.

One could, of course, question the coherence of Kant's example. One could argue, I think correctly, that the supposition that the different substances are the subjects of the successive mental states contradicts the supposition that they really are different substances. Here, of course, one would be accepting a version of the psychological continuity view; one would be maintaining that if S_1 is a subject of mental states existing at time t_1 and S_2 is a subject of mental states existing at time t_2, and if the states of S_1 at t_1 are related to those of S_2 at t_2 in the way Kant supposes, then S_1 and S_2 are one and the same subject of mental states. One could allow, of course, that S_1 at t_1 is composed of different stuff than S_2 at t_2—and if one is a dualist one might even get away with holding that the stuff of which they are composed is immaterial (although speaking of immaterial stuff seems dangerously close to speaking of immaterial matter). In that case one could rewrite Kant's example by saying that there is a succession of different portions of stuff, P_1, P_2 . . . each of which communicates its states to the next. And we could, if we wished, speak of these portions of stuff as 'substances'. But now the successive substances will not themselves be subjects of mental states (any more than, on a materialist view, the different collections of molecules which successively constitute me are subjects of my mental states—what is the subject of mental states is the person which these collections of molecules successively constitute), and there should be no temptation to regard them as persons (or minds).

Locke, like Butler, failed to distinguish clearly between substances in what I will call the Aristotelian sense, the sense in which continuants (like trees) which can survive changes in their composition count as substances, and substances in the sense of portions of stuff (material or immaterial). And this led him to deny that the continued identity of a person requires the continued identity of the same thinking substance. This denial amounts to the claim that the history of a person could be a Kantian succession in which the successive substances are subjects of mental states, and in which each in turn thinks the thoughts of the single person whom they in turn constitute. But once we have distinguished these senses of 'substance', it is clear what Locke ought to have said: it is that the identity of a person requires (trivially) the identity of a substance in the Aristotelian sense, that it does not require the identity of any substance in the portion-of-stuff sense, and that substances in the latter sense are not persons and not subjects of mental states.

15 Conceptual Analysis or Factual Analysis?

I have postponed until now a consideration of the question of how we ought to understand questions and claims about what personal identity 'consists in'. The central issue here is whether such questions and claims are best understood as ones to be answered or assessed by a priori analysis of concepts, or whether they should be understood as factual questions or claims about the world, to be answered or assessed on empirical grounds. (A third possibility, not to be discounted, is that they are partly the first, partly the second.) A similar question arises about functionalist accounts of mind. Must functional definitions be conceptually or analytically true, or can they be synthetic truths which it is perhaps the business of psychologists rather than philosophers to discover? Since the version of the psychological continuity view I favour invokes the functionalist view of mind, I see these issues as very closely related.

Much of the literature on personal identity treats it as a conceptual problem which is to be solved by a priori analysis of concepts. But a variety of factors, including Quinean scepticism about the analytic–synthetic distinction and the many difficulties to which the traditional analyses of personal identity seem subject, have led many philosophers to doubt whether any illuminating and true conceptual analysis of personal identity is to be had. And some of these have held that the question 'What does personal identity consist in?' can nevertheless be given an answer. According to John Mackie, it will be answered by specifying the 'real essence of personal identity'.[46] This will be 'whatever underlies and makes possible the unity of consciousness'. What this real essence is is an empirical question. But, says Mackie, we know at least the outline of the answer: 'what makes co-consciousness possible is the structure of the central nervous system and the persistence of that structure through time'. A similar view has been advanced by John Perry.[47] What a theory of personal identity should try to find, according to

[46]Mackie 1976, p. 200.
[47]Perry 1976a, pp. 69–73.

Perry, is a relation between successive stages of human beings, the 'P-relation', which explains the approximate truth of the generalizations about human beings (individuated by their bodies) which make up what Perry calls 'Human theory'. He suggests that the relation *having the same brain* (thought of as a relation between stages) is a plausible candidate for being the P-relation.

If 'person' were just a name for members of the human species, or (what is not quite the same thing) if all persons were necessarily human beings, then it might be plausible to maintain that something like having the same brain, or the persistence of the central nervous system, is the 'real essence' of personal identity, and what it ultimately 'consists in'. But as was indicated in section 11, that seems not to be so. It does not seem out of the question that Martians who are not of our species should have the right sort of psychological make-up to count as persons. And it seems conceivable that the Martians might differ from us so much physiologically that they have no single organ that could be called a brain. If it is so much as nomologically possible that there should be such creatures (and I think we have no reason to think it is not) then it seems wrong to say that personal identity consists in brain identity (even if *human* personal identity does consist in this).

There is an obvious analogy between the question of what personal identity consists in and the question of what having a certain mental state, e.g., pain, consists in. The sort of answer Mackie and Perry envision as being given to the former question is analogous to that which the psychophysical identity theory gives to the latter. Both might be called 'parochial views'—the one of personal identity, the other of mental states. And both seem open to the same objection. If someone tells us that pain consists in C-fibre firing, it seems appropriate to reply that he has at best told us what pain consists in *in us*, or, better, how it is realized *in us*. What Mackie and Perry have done is to indicate how personal identity (or copersonality, or psychological unity) are realised *in us*, i.e., in members of our own species. And this does not answer the question 'What does personal identity consist in?' at the level of abstractedness at which we want it answered, just as the claim about pain and C-fibres does not answer the question 'What does pain consist in?'

at the level of abstractness at which we want it answered. What we want in the latter case is a specification of the nature of pain which will guide us in finding out what its realization is in particular creatures or species. This is what a functionalist account of mind attempts to give. And something analogous to this is what we want in the case of personal identity. The psychological continuity account sketched earlier seems at least to be at the right level of abstractness; it should apply to the Martians as well as to us, and if Locke's rational parrot is a possibility it ought to apply to it.

It might be objected that no matter how different the Martians are from us physiologically, they will have to have something that amounts to a central nervous system; and that if this is so, Mackie's claim about the 'real' essence of personal identity can be upheld. But I think that this claim is true only if 'amounts to' means 'plays the functional role of'. Certainly it does not seem necessary that the Martians should have something that would look like a nervous system to a dissecting human anatomist. But if we make 'nervous system' a functional notion, we will have to say what the defining functional role is. And then, if Mackie's claim is to be true, specifying this functional role fully would come to nothing less than spelling out the functional natures of mental states, and, what I have claimed this involves, the functional role of psychological unity and copersonality.

But is it not possible that the functional account of mental states, and the associated psychological continuity account of personal identity, could themselves be regarded as giving the 'real essence' of the mental states and personal identity—as opposed to giving their 'nominal essence' (i.e., giving an a priori conceptual analysis)? Perhaps, but I am rather inclined to doubt it. If believing, desiring, remembering, etc. are not to be identified with their human realizations (or rather with disjunctions of these, since there is no reason to think there is just one way in which any of these states or activities is realized even in humans), there seems little reason to think that there *is* a real essence of any of these. And if being a person is not to be identified with membership in a particular biological species, there seems little reason to think that there is a real essence of that either.

David Wiggins has suggested a view, the 'animal attribute' view of personhood, according to which, while persons are not limited to any single biological species, every person necessarily belongs to some species of animals or other, and shares the real essence of that species.[48] On this view, presumably, what the identity of a particular person 'consists in' will depend on what animal species that person belongs to, and will be something to be discovered in the way Mackie and Perry think that the real essence of personal identity is to be discovered. This view assumes something I questioned in section 11, namely that the sense of 'is' in which a person is an animal is the predicative sense. But there is a further difficulty with it if it holds that there is no account of personal identity that it is not species-specific, i.e., which is not simply an account of what the identity of some species of animals consists in. In allowing the possibility of there being persons of different biological species, this view seems committed to some degree of functionalism about mental states.[49] Presumably it will be some sort of psychological specification that collects together different creatures as persons, and if these creatures can be of different species, and differ significantly in their physical make-up, it is hard to see how the conception of the relevant psychological states could be anything but a functionalist one (especially if we assume, as Wiggins does, that dualist accounts are not in the running). But if, as I argued in section 6, there is a psychological continuity account of personal identity implicit in the functional specifications of the various sorts of mental states, then it is impossible to have a functionalist account of what creatures count as persons without having, at least in outline, a psychological continuity account of what the identity of persons (of whatever species) consists in.

[48]Wiggins 1980, p. 171.
[49]Wiggins apparently does not agree—see Wiggins 1980, p. 172ff.

16 The Duplication Argument Revisited

Despite my disparaging remarks in the last section about the 'parochial view' of personal identity, I think that we must acknowledge that our ordinary conception of personal identity, as reflected in our intuitions about possible cases, has a parochial element in it. This comes out in something I temporarily suppressed in my discussion of the duplication argument in section 12.

Consider again the case in which the BST-device misfunctions, and fails to erase the states of brain A when it records them and imposes identical states on brain B. In this case we are (I think) strongly inclined to say that Smith, the pre-transfer A-brain person, continues to exist with the same body and brain, and that the post-transfer B-brain person is simply a newly created duplicate of Smith. But this seems to conflict with the non-branching psychological continuity view; a proponent of that view seems to be obliged to say that since there has been a branching, neither the post-transfer A-brain person nor the post-transfer B-brain person is identical to Smith. What causes trouble here is the 'parochial' intuition that psychological continuity which is carried in the ordinary way by the brain takes precedence over psychological continuity mediated by the BST-procedure.

A way out of the difficulty would be to adopt the still more parochial view that the causal connections between earlier and later stages brought about by the BST-procedure are not causal connections 'of the appropriate kind' to yield memory and other sorts of psychological connectedness, and so do not give us psychological continuity of the relevant sort. This would amount to denying that this case counts as a case of 'branching'. But one cannot say this if one holds, as I am inclined to, that when the BST-device functions properly, and erases the states of the 'donor' brain before imposing them on the 'recipient' brain, the procedure is person-preserving.

What is needed here is a refinement of the non-branching psychological continuity view. Let us distinguish between 'equal' and 'unequal' branching. There are at least two ways in which branching could be unequal. One, which is not what we have in our present example, involves a person-stage at one time having psychological connections with two different person-stages at another time, but (to put it crudely) having many more psychological connections with one than with the other (e.g., a bit of my brain matter is put in your brain, giving you a few memories from the inside of my past life; but you have a much greater memory access to your own past life than you have to mine, and I have a much greater memory access to my past life than you have to mine). In the case of the misfunctioning BST-device we have a different sort of inequality; the inequality stems, not from the amount of psychological connectedness, but from the different sorts of causal mechanisms involved in it. This difference constitutes inequality if we think, as we appparently do, that personal identity, or psychological unity, is somehow better realized in the continued normal functioning of the brain than it is in the operations of the BST-device.

The recognition that our conception of personal identity has this parochial element—that the way personal identity is in fact realized in us is given a privileged status—is compatible with the claim that where the BST-device functions properly its operation is person-preserving. But to reconcile these we need to modify the non-branching provision of the psychological continuity theory into something like Robert Nozick's 'closest continuer theory'.[50] In cases of equal branching we can say, as I said earlier about branching in general, that neither 'offshoot' counts as identical to the original person. In cases of unequal branching, the offshoot that is the 'closest continuer' of the original person counts as identical to him. There will be various dimensions of 'closeness'. The one that concerns us here might be called the dimension of 'aptness of causal mechanism'. In our example, one can hold that if the BST-device functions properly then the closest continuer of Smith is the post-transfer B-brain person, while allowing that if it misfunctions in the way imagined the closest continuer is the post-transfer A-brain person.

If I am asked why I regard the continued normal functioning of the brain as a better realization of psychological unity than the operation of the BST-device, I can give no reason. And I can give no reason why I would prefer (as I now can't help feeling that I

[50]See Nozick 1981.

would) to survive in the ordinary way, with my present brain and body, rather than to have my brain-states transferred to a healthy clone of my body (even assuming that the transfer procedure is sure-fire). I also am not sure that these are attitudes I would continue to have if I lived in the society imagined in section 10, where the BST-device plays a central role in people's lives. And I cannot see that I would be in any way irrational if I changed these attitudes and became like the people in that society. What I feel quite confident of is that there is no *metaphysical* consideration which provides a valid reason for having attitudes towards personal identity and survival which are 'parochial' to the extent these attitudes are.

Richard Swinburne's Reply

Shoemaker's very clear 'psychological continuity' account of personal identity seems to me to fail to take seriously the possibility (described in my essay on pp. 17ff) that a person may not suffer the sufferings or enjoy the joys of some person psychologically continuous with himself. This is no mere logical possibility but in brain splitting and brain-state transfer (BST) cases a very serious epistemic possibility. I illustrated it from a brain splitting case where two persons both had the apparent memories and character of an original person and were caused to do so by having part of his brain, and so were realizations of psychological continuity of a very close kind (see Shoemaker's essay, pp. 130ff). If apparent in that case the possibility should be even more evident in the BST cases.

There may well be, as Shoemaker supposes, some reason for supposing that a society, in which BST is common, means by 'person' (pp. 109f) 'what we mean by it'. But in that case there is good reason for anyone who reflects on the issue to doubt whether 'the BST procedure is person-preserving', even if that society unthinkingly supposes that it is. Many societies have believed that present persons are their dead ancestors reincarnated. The fact that the society does hold that view about personal identity has no tendency to show that that view is true and the same goes for any society which holds the view that the BST-procedure is person-preserving. For it may occur to an intelligent member of the society, and will certainly occur to the outsider, that the society is committed to the view that whether P_2 at the later time t_2 is identical with a previous person P_1 at t_1 depends, not merely on facts about those persons, but on whether there happens to have survived up to t_2 any other person P_2^* who is a 'closer continuer' of P_1 (e.g., not merely does he have brain-states causally dependent on those of P_1 but has the same brain as P_1), and so that who P_2 is depends on what happens in a body quite other than P_2's (viz., P_2^*'s). But surely there is a fact about who P_2 is (whether he is a certain individual who could be picked out by a rigid designator) which is quite independent of what happens to someone else. Whether I am the President of the US in 1982 may indeed depend on circumstances far beyond myself, but whether I am Swinburne (i.e., the same person as a certain past person called 'Swinburne') cannot depend on things quite outside myself. Or as I emphasized in the example quoted by Shoemaker on p. 118, a theory which claims that I survive only if there is one 'closest continuer' of me in future has the absurd consequence that the way to ensure my own survival is to kill someone else. If the society became conscious of these absurdities, it might well abandon its way of talking.

Shoemaker's response is that these consequences of the society's way of talking are not really absurd. They appear so only if we make the false assumption that what we are concerned about when we are concerned about our own survival is the future existence of a person identical with ourselves. Shoemaker writes that his 'natural' (p. 119) assumption can be questioned. What we are really concerned about is the future well-being of persons psychologically continuous with ourselves. In normal life today there is only one future person psychologically continuous with a given person, and that person is identical with him. Hence the confusion. But where there is brain splitting and BST, psychological continuity may exist without personal identity. Our concern being with persons psychologically continuous with ourselves, we see that the fact that some future person is not me, need in no way diminish the peculiar kind of concern I have for his future well-being. When we bear that in mind, Shoemaker claims, we see that the above consequences are not absurd. Of course we may have a moral or altruistic concern with the well-being of future persons other than ourselves. But what Shoemaker is claiming is that the selfish concern which we have for our own future is really a concern for anyone psychologically continuous with ourselves.

This seems just false. For psychological continuity being as Shoemaker acknowledges, a matter of degree, the kind of selfish concern which we have for future persons psychologically continuous with ourselves ought to vary with the strength of the continuity. I ought to be more concerned with someone who has qualitatively identical brain states to mine caused by mine, but even more concerned about someone who has these and also has my brain (see Shoemaker's essay, p. 115 example). But selfish concern can only be focused on one person and in this example it will be focused on the person who has my brain. If I am selfish, I shall be quite indifferent to the fate of the other person, even though he is psychologically continuous with myself. My desire for happiness in the world to come is not in the least satisfied by the knowledge that archangels normally produce a duplicate of each dead person (with his apparent memories and character). To satisfy my desire, I want something more—that I enjoy what that future person enjoys and so I be he. The only reason why 'the future sufferings and delights' of a person psychologically continuous with myself 'cannot be a matter of indifference' to me, is because I take psychological continuity as fallible evidence of something else, viz., personal identity; I suspect that, in addition to being psychologically continuous with him, I will suffer his sufferings and enjoy his joys. The less reason there is to suspect that (e.g., where the future person is produced by a mechanism which could easily produce a thousand others, which were even closer continuers of myself, by having more atoms from my brain), the less will be my selfish concern for that future person.

Certainly the Kantian series of substances (pp. 123f) is a logical possibility, but one which we have good occasion to believe not to occur—for the reasons stated in my section 4 (e.g., we have reason for relying on apparent memory to tell us which past person we were).

Shoemaker's case for his own theory is that the psychological continuity account of personal identity is entailed by a functionalist theory of mental states. That may be so. The trouble is that, as Shoemaker admits, the functionalist theory of mental states is 'widely disputed'. Indeed, the theory seems to me certainly false.

As Shoemaker states it (p. 92), the core of functionalism is that 'every mental state is a "functional state", i.e., a state which is definable in terms of its relations (primarily its causal relations) to sensory inputs, behaviourial outputs, and (especially) other functional states. A mental state is individuated, and constituted as being the particular mental state it is, by its place in a complex causal network of states.' The other functional states in terms of which a given functional state is defined are themselves ultimately to be defined in terms of sensory input and behavioural output. Studying the sensory input and behavioural output of a person, we construct a system of beliefs and desires which will explain that behaviour as simply as possible. The trouble is that for any given stretch of a person's sensory input and behavioural output you can construct alternative systems of beliefs and desires which will explain it. I give £10 to a charity having been shown evidence both that the charity will benefit the poor and that my giving will cause me to be respected. My action can be explained either by the belief that my giving will benefit the poor and my desire to benefit the poor, or by the belief that my giving will cause me to be respected, and my desire to be respected. Given that beliefs and desires change with time, we can construct whole alternative theories of the beliefs and desires which a person had at different stages of his life, and which arose from his sensory input and caused his behavioural output. Some such theories may be simpler than others (e.g., ones postulating constant or slowly changing desires rather than suddenly changing desires), and for that reason more likely to be true.

Functionalism is committed to the view that the true account of a person's beliefs and desires is the outside observer's account in terms of the simplest (or on some other grounds best) theory of the person's sensory input and behavioural output. But the person himself knows what he is about, what purposes he is intending to achieve by his actions; that is, to use the functionalist's preferred term 'desire', the person knows which desire is motivating his behaviour. When persons perform intentional actions, they seek to achieve thereby goals of which they are conscious. Hence an agent has knowledge of his desires, or as I would prefer to say, his purposes. And his account of his purposes may conflict with that given by the outsider's best theory of his behaviour. Even if you suppose that agents do not have infallible knowledge of their purposes, and that they may on occasion be mistaken about what they are seeking, clearly they are in a better position to know about them than are outside observers—for they can know everything about their sensory input and behavioural output, which outsiders can know—and something else vital as well. (Since it is they who are seeking to bring about their chosen goals, they must have some direct awareness of what they are seeking.) A person who knows his purposes, knows at any rate his beliefs about how to secure those purposes. I come to a fork in the road and take the road to the left. I have, and know that I have, the purpose of going home. Hence I have, and know that I have, the belief that the road to the left leads home. For if I did not have that belief, I would not have taken that road with the purpose of going home.

Since agents are in a better position to know about their purposes and beliefs than are outside observers, it follows that the best theory about an agent's purposes (or desires) and beliefs constructed by observers from a study of the agent's sensory input and behavioural output may be mistaken. Hence functionalism is mistaken in claiming that every mental state is definable in terms of its causal relations to observable states. There is more to belief and desire than their manifestation in the public world.[1]

Functionalists most usually attempt to make their account of mental states plausible by providing such an account of belief and desire. Even for belief and desire, we have just seen, functionalism will not work. Functionalism is even less plausible as an account of mental states of other kinds, e.g., sensations. There is the notorious problem of the inverted spectrum. Imagine a person who has, relative to me, an inverted spectrum of colour sensations. Whenever he looks at an object which we call 'red' and which causes in me a sensation which I call 'red' it produces in him a sensation which I would call 'blue' if I had it, but which he calls 'red'. Conversely what I call 'blue' produces in him a sensation which I would call 'red'. And so on, for other pairs of colours. He and I have exactly similar patterns of behaviour, reacting to public coloured objects in the same way. He classifies as 'red' the same objects as I do; and he classifies as 'blue' the same objects as I do. And yet our sensations on the occasion when we see objects which we classify in the same way are quite different. A sensation is not 'constituted as being the particular mental state it is, by its place in a complex causal network of states'. As with beliefs and purposes, the best inference to the sensations of another from a

[1]For much more detailed discussion of the nature of belief, see Swinburne, 1981a, ch. 1.

study of his sensory input (in the sense of input, e.g., of light waves, to his sense organs) and behavioural output, may lead us to attribute to others sensations which they do not have.

Since functionalism is a mistaken theory of mind, the fact that it fits naturally with a theory of personal identity in terms of psychological continuity, gives reason to doubt the latter rather than to affirm it.

Sydney Shoemaker's Reply

Despite our disagreement on the central issues, there are many points of agreement between Professor Swinburne and myself. We are in basic agreement on one part of what might be called the epistemology of personal identity. By and large we agree about what are the most basic sorts of evidence of personal identity, and about what various possible phenomena would show or tend to show with regard to questions of personal identity. (Where we disagree is in our views about the source or basis of the evidential principles we agree on.) We also agree in allowing as conceivable, and possible, various things (body switching, disembodied existence, and the like) which many other philosophers have claimed to be inconceivable or impossible.

One difference between us is that Swinburne is a dualist and I am a materialist. But this difference should not be misunderstood. Swinburne's account is avowedly a dualist account. But while mine is a materialist's account (since I am a materialist), it is not as such a materialist account. It is deliberately devised, as is the functionalist account of mind which it incorporates, to be neutral as to how personal identity and mental phenomena are realized—it is neutral as to what sort of matter they are realized in, and even as to whether they are realized in matter at all, as opposed to being realized in the states of some sort of immaterial substance. So while my account is compatible with materialism, it is also compatible with dualism. It is because I believe that there is an acceptable account of mind and personal identity that is compatible with materialism, *and* because I believe that there are independent reasons (roughly, the explanatory success of the physical sciences) for believing materialism to be true, that I am a materialist.

Another difference between Swinburne and myself, and perhaps a more basic one, is that (to put it roughly in the terminology Swinburne takes from Derek Parfit) he holds the 'simple view' of personal identity while I hold the 'complex view'. Part of what Swinburne means by the 'simple view' is that personal identity is something 'ultimate' and 'indefinable'.

The simple view denies all versions of what Swinburne calls the 'empiricist theory' of personal identity, and apparently denies that it is possible to give any sort of non-trivial and non-circular analysis of personal identity—any account of what the truth of statements of personal identity 'consists in'. But apparently it is also part of the simple view, as Swinburne conceives it, that personal identity does not admit of borderline cases; he thinks that questions of personal identity always have answers, whether or not we have any way of discovering them. It should be clear from my essay that I think that it is possible to give a non-trivial and non-circular analysis of personal identity. I also think that personal identity admits of borderline cases. So I reject both parts of Swinburne's simple view, which presumably makes me a proponent of the complex view.[1] However, mine is not an 'empiricist' theory, if by that is meant a theory which does not distinguish the meaning of statements of personal identity from the evidence that supports them, or which analyses the former in terms of the latter in a 'verificationist' manner.

What is the relation between Swinburne's dualism and his acceptance of the simple view? If I am right in claiming that my own view is compatible with dualism, then it cannot be the case that dualism implies the simple view. Does the simple view imply dualism? It would not imply it, I think, if it consisted only in the indefinability thesis—the view that personal identity cannot be given a non-trivial analysis. For there are philosophers who think that the indefinability thesis holds also for the identity of trees, stones, and automobiles, and presumably these philosophers are not committed to dualism about *such* entities. What might more plausibly be thought to lead to dualism is the determinacy thesis—the thesis that statements of personal identity always have determinate truth values, and that personal identity does not admit of borderline cases. If one thinks that there are possible circumstances in which there is no room in the *physical* world for a 'fact of the matter' that would bestow a determinate truth value on a particular statement of personal identity, but nevertheless thinks that there has to be a fact of the matter that does this, one must locate this fact of the

[1]There is more than this, I think, to what Parfit calls the complex view. See Parfit 1971a.

matter elsewhere than in the physical world. I will return to the determinacy thesis later; right now I want to consider the case for dualism Swinburne makes in his section 2.

In the opening pages of this section Swinburne lumps together claims which it is important for me to distinguish. He says that there is no contradiction or incoherence in the supposition of someone's changing bodies, and even in the supposition of someone's existing disembodied. He also says, as if it were the same sort of point, that it is not logically impossible for a person to continue to exist without any apparent memory of his previous doings. As just expressed, the latter claim is one hardly anyone would disagree with; and some of his formulations make it something no one would disagree with—as when he says that it is not logically necessary that a person 'have certain apparent memories, if he is to be the person he is' (p. 25). But I think that it is clear that he means to be asserting something much stronger than this—he means to be asserting that it is not logically necessary that the successive stages of a person's life be linked by any of the kinds of relations which psychological continuity theories (like mine) make constitutive of personal identity. With this of course I disagree. In lumping these claims together Swinburne rather suggests that the same sorts of considerations serve at once to establish dualism and to refute the complex view, i.e., to refute all of the sorts of theories Swinburne classifies as 'empiricist'. But the claims, and the arguments based on them, need to be distinguished. As I am about to show, the first claim, while I think that it is true, does not (contrary to what Swinburne supposes) give any support to dualism. The second claim, on the other hand, would refute the complex view if it were true (on the strong interpretation of it Swinburne intends). But as I shall argue, Swinburne has no good reason for thinking that it is true.

I begin with the argument for dualism. Swinburne thinks that it is possible that he should cease to have a body at a certain time and continue to exist after that time. According to his 'wider Aristotelian principle', this would not be possible if he were, prior to ceasing to have a body, a purely material being; for in that case there would not be the continuity of composition between his pre-disembodiment self and his post-disembodiment self which the wider Aristotelian principle requires. He must therefore be made at least in part of some non-bodily stuff, a soul, which can persist through the loss of his body.

Let me first observe that the wider Aristotelian principle seems far from self-evident. One way for a materialist to reject Swinburne's argument would be to reject that principle. (He would have to reject it if he believed, as I am inclined to, that the 'brain-state transfer procedure' described in section 10 of my essay could be person-preserving—for in that procedure there is no continuity of stuff across the transfer.) However, I shall assume for the sake of discussion that the principle is true, and will show that even on that assumption the argument fails.

In an attempt to dispel any suspicion that his argument commits a modal fallacy, Swinburne lays the argument out formally in a footnote. I agree that the argument commits no modal fallacy, and is in fact valid (in the sense that its premises entail its conclusion). Assuming the wider Aristotelian principle, whether the argument is sound depends on whether its initial premise, namely the claim that he (Swinburne) could survive instantaneous disembodiment, is true. (I speak here of 'instantaneous' disembodiment, because it does seem compatible with the wider Aristotelian principle that a purely material being should gradually change into an immaterial one, unless we assume, as Swinburne seems to me to do without argument, that immaterial substances are always indivisable.) And there does seem to be a modal fallacy, or at any rate a confusion about modality, in the reasoning used in the text to support that premise.

As we have noted, Swinburne begins his section with the claim that there is no contradiction in supposing that a person might acquire a totally new body and that it is equally coherent to suppose that a person might become disembodied. I accept the first of these claims, and with reservations that needn't concern us here I also accept the second. Notice that these are not claims of *de re* possibility.[2] The second does not assert concerning any particular thing that it is possible that *it* should become disembodied. If it asserts any possibility at all, it asserts

---

[2] A claim of *de re* possibility claims concerning a particular thing (*res*) that such-and-such is possible with respect to it; such claims are distinguished from statements of *de dicto* possibility, in which the truth of some proposition (*dictum*), which may contain no reference to any particular thing, is said to be possible.

the possibility that there should be a person who undergoes disembodiment—and it is entirely compatible with the possibility of this that all actual persons should be essentially embodied and so incapable of becoming disembodied (this would be so if the wider Aristotelian principle were true, and if all actual persons were composed entirely of matter). Yet a few pages later (p. 29) we find Swinburne asserting, with no additional argument, that 'for any present person who is presently conscious, there is no logical impossibility . . . that that person continue to exist without his body', and using this claim together with the wider Aristotelian principle to argue for dualism. It is important to see that this latter claim is in no way supported by those earlier ones about what we can suppose without contradiction or incoherence. To suppose that it follows from them is like supposing that from the fact that there could be someone who could beat the current heavyweight boxing champion of the world it follows that *I* could beat the current heavyweight boxing champion of the world.

But perhaps Swinburne didn't intend to support his crucial premise with his earlier claim about the logical coherence of supposing that 'a person' might become disembodied; perhaps he thinks it is established directly by the Cartesian thought-experiment of imagining *oneself* existing disembodied. But what do I do when I contemplate the supposition of *my* becoming disembodied that is different from what I do when I contemplate in the abstract the supposition that *someone* might exist disembodied? Well, perhaps I imagine (or try to imagine) what it would be like to be or become disembodied; instead of considering the kind of evidence (seances, etc.) that might persuade us that someone else now exists disembodied, I try to imagine what the experience of a disembodied person would be like. But whatever I do, how would it support a claim of *de re* possibility to the effect that I am something that could cease to be embodied without ceasing to exist? At best I will find that there is no logical or conceptual incoherence involved in the supposition that someone whose situation is epistemically like mine, someone having all of the properties I *know* myself to have, should become disembodied. This perhaps establishes that it is 'epistemically possible' that I should become disembodied (where 'It is epistemically possible that P' means 'P is compatible with what I know'). But epistemic possibility is obviously not what Swinburne needs.

In general, it is quite hopeless to suppose that a claim of *de re* possibility, a claim to the effect that some actually existing thing could undergo such-and-such changes, can be grounded on mere thought-experiments, or on considerations of what can be supposed or imagined without logical or conceptual incoherence. And anyone who thinks that this can be done should realize that it is not open to Swinburne to hold this; for the view that this can be done contradicts Swinburne's Aristotelian principle. Suppose that up until noon today a particular object O, say a statue, contains no gold. And suppose that I do not realize this. In whatever sense Swinburne can imagine becoming disembodied, I will be able to imagine O's coming at noon to be composed entirely of gold. Certainly I will be able to imagine something having all of the properties I know O to have (just before noon) coming at noon to be composed entirely of gold. And no doubt it is possible that some such thing should undergo such a change (e.g., if just prior to noon it is composed *almost* entirely of gold). But the Aristotelian principle says that this cannot happen to O. Like the Cartesian principle that whatever is a purely material thing is essentially so, the Aristotelian principle implies that there are statements of *de re* necessity and impossibility whose epistemological status is that of being a posteriori (empirical) rather than a priori, and which cannot be refuted by mere thought-experiments, i.e., by considerations about what can be imagined without conceptual absurdity. Anyone who holds either of these principles cannot consistently argue from the imaginability of disembodiment to dualism; at most the imaginability of this shows that it is possible that there should be minded creatures of which dualism is true—it does not show that it is true of any of the minded creatures there actually are.[3] Since the Aristotelian principle is a premise of Swinburne's argument, the argument is internally incoherent.

While thought-experiments cannot be used to establish claims of *de re* possibility, they can legitimately be used to test, and sometimes refute, claims about what is conceptually necessary and sufficient for something—e.g., for personal

[3]See Shoemaker 1983.

identity. Unfortunately, however, Swinburne seems to suppose that the thought-experiments that refute certain simple-minded versions of the memory continuity theory of personal identity suffice to refute all versions of the 'complex view' which make personal identity consist in some sort of psychological continuity. He bases his rejection of such theories on the intelligibility of certain stories, such as that about the waters of Lethe, which make a person forget all of his previous life. But while I agree that we find intelligible the idea of a person losing all personal memories, or all event memories (especially if this is what in my essay I call 'ordinary' rather than 'philosophical' amnesia), it is quite another thing to claim that we find intelligible the idea of a person surviving in such a way that there is no psychological connectedness of any kind between his earlier and his later states. The latter is not what happens in the stories people find intelligible. (There are of course stories whose charm depends precisely on the fact that they give a semblance of intelligibility to what is in fact logically impossible.)

I want now to focus on one aspect of Swinburne's view that personal identity is 'ultimate', namely what I have called the 'determinacy thesis'. This has been well put by Derek Parfit, who rejects it, as the thesis that questions about personal identity must have answers even in cases in which 'though we know the answer to every other question, we have no idea how to answer a question of personal identity'.[4] Swinburne seems to think that opposition to this view, such as he finds in Wittgenstein's *Blue Book*, must stem from verificationist views about meaning, and he devotes considerable space to arguing that there is no defensible version of verificationism which would support such a claim. But verificationism seems to me to be a red herring here. As Parfit observes, no one holds the determinacy thesis about the identity of such things as nations and machines—or, to add some examples to his, such things as clouds and lakes.[5] We are prepared to allow that with such

[4] Parfit 1971b, p. 3.

[5] This needs to be qualified. Nathan Salmon has given an argument that *seems* to establish the determinacy thesis for all kinds of entities. See Salmon 1981. The argument is as follows. Suppose that for a particular a and b there is no fact of the matter as to whether a is identical to b. Then the ordered pair $\langle a,b \rangle$ has the property of being such that there is no fact of the matter whether its first member is identical to its second

things there can be borderline cases, cases in which there is 'no fact of the matter' whether we have one and the same nation, cloud or lake at two different times or places. Swinburne himself seems to allow this, although he tends to conflate the true claim that the identity conditions for such things have some indeterminacy, and so allow for borderline cases, with the (I think) incoherent claim that the identity of such things varies in degree.[6] Presumably it is not verifcationism that leads people (including Swinburne) to reject the determinacy thesis as applied to clouds and the like. And so it need not be verificationism that leads someone to reject it as applied to persons. Indeed, the fact that the view is false for other sorts of things is itself a good prima facie reason to think that it is false for persons. For why should the case of persons be special

member. Clearly the ordered pair $\langle a,a \rangle$ does not have this property (and likewise the ordered pair $\langle b,b \rangle$). But it follows from this and set theory that a is not identical to b. And this contradicts the original assumption that there is no fact of the matter whether a is identical to b. Since the assumption (together with set theory) entails its own denial, it is necessarily false.

The argument is sound, but its conclusion, properly understood, does not contradict what I think has been typically meant by the claim that there are cases in which there is no fact of the matter whether an identity holds. The claim is best put by saying that identity statements sometimes lack determinate truth value even though the terms in them do (in a sense) refer. What makes the claim true, in a way that doesn't contradict what Salmon establishes, is the fact that the vagueness of general terms can result in indeterminacy of reference, and that where it is indeterminate which of several things a term in an identity statement refers to, it may be indeterminate whether that statement is true. If, for example, the vagueness of the term 'building' makes it indeterminate whether Alpha Hall and Beta Hall should count as parts of the same building (they are connected by a rather flimsy covered walkway) it may be indeterminate whether the identity statement 'The building in which Smith is lecturing is the same as the building in which Jones is lecturing' is true, if Smith is lecturing in Alpha Hall and Jones is lecturing in Beta Hall. Since vagueness has to do with the fit between language, or concepts, and the world, and not with the nature of the things in the world as such, this is not a case in which an ordered pair of things in the world has the impossible property of being such that there is no fact of the matter as to whether its first member is identical to its second.

[6]Swinburne attributes the view that personal identity is a matter of degree to Derek Parfit, and seems himself to endorse the view that the identity of things other than persons is a matter of degree. It is true that Parfit says that personal identity is 'in its nature' a matter of degree; but he also says that it is 'in its logic all or nothing' (Parfit 1971a, p. 685). I take it that saying that in its nature it is a matter of degree is just a (I think misleading) way of saying that the relations that constitute it, i.e., psychological connectedness of various kinds, can vary in degree. It is compatible with this that it makes no sense to say that something is more or less, or to some extent, (numerically) identical to something, and I take it that Parfit acknowledges this in what he says about the 'logic' of personal identity. A slight qualification is needed here; one can say that a is to some extent identical to b if this means that a is *partly* identical to b, i.e., that part of a is identical to part of b. But this has no relevant application to persons.

in this respect? I think that the explanation of how statements about the identity of clouds can be indeterminate in truth value would have to involve the fact that 'cloud' is to some extent a vague term. The vagueness of a general term 'G' can result in indeterminacy of reference in definite descriptions containing it ('the cloud I am pointing at'), and where there is such indeterminacy of reference there is the possibility of indeterminacy of truth value in identity statements involving such descriptions. (See the building example in footnote 5 of this reply.) On any psychologically plausible theory of reference it is to be expected that the sortal terms in our language will be to some extent vague. And there is no reason to think that 'person' is an exception.

Swinburne lays considerable stress on the fact that 'the continuing existence of a person over time is often something experienced by that person' (p. 45). He also stresses that 'among the data of experience are . . . that certain simultaneous experiences are the experiences of a common subject' (p. 45). If the claim that the unity of experience (both diachronic and synchronic) can itself be 'experienced by' the subject of the experiences means that the subject's knowledge of this unity is often non-inferential, not inferred from something 'more ultimate' (p. 45), this is something I also stress in my essay, and something of which I made a great deal in an earlier work (see Shoemaker 1963, chs 3 and 4). Later on I will quibble a bit with the way Swinburne expresses part of this claim, but the claim is one with which I fundamentally agree.

What is very difficult for me to see is how Swinburne thinks that this point about a person's awareness of his own identity, or of the unity of his experience, supports his dualism and his view that personal identity is 'ultimate' and 'unanalysable'. He must, I think, be relying on some principle to the effect that if the fact that P consists in, is analysable into, the fact that XYZ, it is impossible for anyone to come to know that P without inferring it from the fact that XYZ. But this is a principle that I see no reason to believe. It seems perfectly compatible with the supposition that so-and-so's being true of a person consists in something complex, and is something that others can know about that person only inferentially, that persons should be so constructed (by God, or by natural selection) that when so-and-so is true of a person this automatically results in that person's believing that so-and-so is true of him—and that such beliefs count as knowledge because of the reliable way in which they are produced. (See section 8 of my essay.) I do not wish to minimize the difficulty of giving a satisfactory account of self-awareness. But I do not see that dualist theories of mind promise to be any more successful at accounting for the peculiarities of self-awareness (e.g., the non-inferential and incorrigible character of much of it) than materialist theories. To appeal to the alleged unanalysability of persons, or of personal identity, is not to solve the problem, but just to sweep it under the rug.

Now for my quibble about Swinburne's formulation of the claim about the awareness we have of our own identity over time. As I argue in my essay, given that 'fission' of persons is a logical possibility, a person's direct awareness of the diachronic unity of his experiences is not as such knowledge that the experiences belong to the same person, and so is not as such knowledge of 'the continued existence of a person over time'; it yields such knowledge only when combined with the presumption (which given our knowledge of the world it is always reasonable to make) that the experiences in question were not separated by an episode of fission or fusion (more generally, by an episode of branching). I claim this to be so even of the awareness (which Swinburne discusses) of one experience being immediately followed by another; for if fission were to occur in the middle of such a temporally extended awareness then the awareness itself would undergo fission and the later parts of it would not be copersonal either with each other or with the earlier part (and so the immediately post-fission awareness of the immediately pre-fission experience has to be treated as like memory, or quasi-memory,[7] awareness, despite the phenomenological facts that

[7]On p. 56 of his essay Swinburne gives a mistaken account of the notion of 'quasi-remembering' (or what has sometimes been called 'q-remembering') which I introduced in my paper 'Persons and their Pasts' (1970a). He characterizes a quasi-memory as 'an ordinary personal memory minus the belief that the subject himself did the deeds or had the experiences'. As I use the term, all ordinary memories count as quasi-memories; indeed, if remembering is analysed as I suggest in section 4 of my essay in this volume, there is no difference at all between remembering and quasi-remembering. When I first introduced the term, I took it to be analytic of 'remembering' that one can only remember one's own past; the notion of quasi-remembering was then introduced to cover cases in which someone has to past actions and experiences other than his own an access that is otherwise just like remembering (and to cover cases of remembering as a special case). I now prefer to define 'remember' in such a way as to allow the logical possibility of someone (veridically) remembering, from the inside, actions and experiences other than his own.

make it plausible to speak here of awareness of a 'specious present'). To be sure Swinburne claims to have arguments that show the impossibility of fission and fusion. But in fact he has no argument at all against the impossibility of what I mean by fission (likewise for fusion), and indeed seems to accept it. What I mean is the possibility of a situation—exemplified by the double half-brain transplant example which Swinburne himself uses—in which two later person-stages are connected to a single earlier stage by the sorts of psychological relationships that ordinarily link only the successive stages of a single person. I think Swinburne takes the claim that fission is possible to mean that in such a case the later persons (the 'offshoots') are in some sense identical to the original person; but that is not what I mean by it.

In the final section of his essay Swinburne discusses the nature of our evidence of personal identity. I agree with him about the primacy of the memory criterion of personal identity *vis-à-vis* such evidence of personal identity as brain identity, bodily continuity, fingerprint similarity, and the like. And I like his view that the connection between memory continuity and continuity of character has an a priori basis, and is not merely an empirical connection (that there is such an intimate connection between the two, it should be noted, is just what one should expect on a functionalist account of mind of the sort I advance in my essay). I also accept Swinburne's 'principle of credulity'. But what I take to be the central claim of that section, namely that our use of apparent memory as a criterion of personal identity is 'a special unavoidable case of application of the principle of credulity', seems to me to be mistaken. Let me show why.

Imagine someone, call him Tom, who was brought up with the belief that fission frequently occurs, and that therefore the fact that one remembers a past action or experience 'from the inside' does not make it certain that the subject of that past action or experience was oneself. A memory that any of us would spontaneously express (if it were his) by saying 'I remember hitting him', or 'I remember that I hit him', Tom would spontaneously express by saying something like 'I remember from the inside the (or a) hitting of him'. And in such a case he would not believe that he himself had been the subject of the action in question, unless provided with evidence that no fission had occurred in his mental history during the interval in question. Now suppose that Tom reports a past action in this way, that we know independently that such an action was in fact done (that what he seems to remember did in fact happen), and that we know, although he does not, that in fact fission does not occur (at least not in this part of the world). In this case our judgement that Tom is (one and the same person as) the person who did the past action would be grounded on considerations of memory. Now in taking it that Tom does remember what he seems to remember we can, if you like, be said to be invoking the principle of credulity. But this gives no support to Swinburne's claim, since to say that Tom really does remember (or quasi-remember) that action from the inside is not yet to make any claim of personal identity. And when we do go on to make the identity claim, concluding it from the fact that he remembers the action from the inside plus the fact that there has been no relevant branching, the principle of credulity is not being invoked—what is required to justify that inference is not the principle of credulity (which is powerless to do so) but a substantive principle relating memory and personal identity. But our grounds for this judgement of personal identity would be every bit as good as—indeed, they would be essentially the same as—they would have been if Tom had actually claimed to remember that he did the past action, instead of making the weaker claim that he remembers the action from the inside. For Tom will not, in general, be in a better position than we are to know that the inference from the weaker claim to the stronger claim is justified. So we can conclude that in general the use of considerations of memory as evidence of personal identity is not just an application of the principle of credulity.

It is obvious that Swinburne's attempt to exhibit the use of the memory criterion as an application of the principle of credulity is motivated by a desire to undermine the idea that the primacy of the memory criterion shows that personal identity consists, at least in part, in facts about memory. His attempt fails, as I have shown. But quite apart from the objection I have just raised, there seems to me something profoundly mistaken about the sharp divorce Swinburne apparently wants to effect between epistemology and metaphysics—in this case, between the question of how personal identity is known, and the question of what it consists in. If one believes that the principle of credulity is a correct epistemological principle, one must also believe that the world is such (and, among other things, persons are such) that reliance on this principle is a reliable way of acquiring knowledge. It is easy to concoct theories of personal identity (not ones that anyone has ever held) that have the consequence that the use of the principle of credulity is not reliable—that it systematically takes us from true premises (the evidence of what people say) to false conclusions. That a theory has this consequence is of course a reason for rejecting it. We also would have ample reason for rejecting an account of personal identity if it implied evidential principles about personal identity that are systematically at odds with those we actually apply. Other theories are objectionable, not because they imply mistaken claims about the epistemology of personal identity, but because they leave it an unexplained mystery that the things we count as evidence of personal identity really are good evidence of it. Swinburne's theory seems to me to fall into this category. A satisfactory theory of personal identity ought to explain how it is that the things we take to be evidence really are evidence, and should explain such facts as the priority of the memory criterion relative to (say) the fingerprint criterion. It is to be hoped that it would also explain, or help to explain, the reliability of the principle of credulity (although, as I have shown, explaining this is not the same thing as explaining the epistemology of personal identity). A theory of the sort Swinburne offers is powerless to explain any of these things. And as far as I can see, the only sort of theory that has any hope of explaining them is a functionalist/psychological continuity theory of the sort sketched in my essay.

The main criticisms Swinburne makes of theories like my own are, I think, anticipated and answered in my essay (at the time of writing this, of course, I have not seen whatever additional criticisms he makes in his comments on my main essay). But I must protest his repeated implication in his section 1 that according to the complex view 'mere logic' (p. 18), or 'a mere philosophical analysis of the concept of personal identity' (p. 20), can tell you 'which experiences will be yours tomorrow'. That would indeed be a silly view—but it is a view which nobody has held. What the complex view says is that where such questions have answers (which need not be always), their answers are determined, not by 'mere' logic alone, or by a 'mere' analysis of personal identity alone, but by these *together with the relevant empirical facts*—e.g., facts about the sorts of causal connections that obtain between certain experiences and certain other experiences. And Swinburne has not shown that there is anything silly about that. Swinburne's own view appears to be that such questions always have answers, and that the answers are underdetermined by, indeed (if I correctly understand him) logically independent of, all of the facts that can be described without the use of the notion of personal identity. That, of course, I deny (but see section 7 of my essay for the necessary qualifications).

Bibliography

A valuable collection of important classical and recent writings on the subject of personal identity, useful for those beginning its study, is Perry 1975a (see below).

Aquinas, St Thomas, *Summa contra Gentiles*, II, 56, 57, 68, 70, 79, 80, 81. Translated under the title *On the Truth of the Catholic* Faith, Book II translated by James F. Anderson, New York, 1956.

Aquinas, St Thomas, *Summa Theologiæ*.

Aristotle, *De Anima*, Books II and III, translated with an introduction and notes by D. W. Hamlyn, Oxford, 1968.

Aristotle, *Metaphysics*, Book 7.

Berkeley, George, *Principles of Human Knowledge*.

Butler, Joseph, 'Of Personal Identity', in J. H. Bernard (ed.), *The Works of Bishop Butler*, Volume II, London, 1900. Also reprinted in Perry 1975a.

Cartwright, Helen 1970: 'Quantities', *The Philosophical Review*, 79, pp. 25–42.

Chisholm, R. M. 1957: *Perceiving*, Ithaca, NY.

Chisholm, R. M. 1969: 'The Loose and Popular and the Strict and Philosophical Senses of Identity', in N. S. Care and R. H. Grimm (eds), *Perception and Personal Identity*, Cleveland, Ohio.

Danto, A. C. 1965: 'Basic Actions', *American Philosophical Quarterly*, 2, pp. 141–8.

Davidson, Donald 1969: 'Truth and Meaning', in J. W. Davis *et al.* (eds), *Philosophical Logic*, Dordrecht.

Descartes, René, *Meditations on the First Philosophy*, in *The Philosophical Works of Descartes*, Volume I, translated by E. S. Haldane and G. R. T. Ross, Cambridge, 1911.

Deutscher, Max, and C. B. Martin 1966: 'Remembering', *The Philosophical Review*, 75, pp. 161–97.

Foster, John 1979: 'In *Self*-Defence', in G. F. MacDonald (ed.), *Perception and Identity*, London, 1979.

Geach, Peter 1967: 'Identity', *Review of Metaphysics*, XXI, pp. 3–12.

Grice, H. P. 1941: '*Personal Identity*', Mind, 50, pp. 330–50. Reprinted in Perry 1975a.

Hirsch, Eli 1982: *The Concept of Identity*, New York.

Hume, David, *An Enquiry Concerning Human Understanding*, ed. L. A. Selby-Bigge, second edition, Oxford, 1902.

Hume, David, *A Treatise of Human Nature*, ed. L. A. Selby-Bigge, Oxford, 1888. Book I, Part IV, Section VI, 'Of Personal

Identity', and part of the Appendix are reprinted in Perry 1975a.

Kant, Immanuel, *Critique of Pure Reason*, translated by Norman Kemp Smith, New York, 1929.

Kitcher, Patricia 1982: 'Kant on Self-Identity', *The Philosophical Review*, 91, pp. 41–72.

Knox, John Jr 1969: 'Can the Self Survive the Death of its Mind?', *Religious Studies*, 5, pp. 85–97.

Kripke, Saul 1980: *Naming and Necessity*, Oxford, and Cambridge, Mass.

Lewis, David 1966: 'An Argument for the Identity Theory', *Journal of Philosophy*, 63, pp. 17–25.

Lewis, David 1972: 'Psychophysical and Theoretical Identifications', *Australasian Journal of Philosophy*, 50, pp. 249–58.

Lewis, David 1976: 'Survival and Identity', in Amélie Rorty (ed.), *The Identities of Persons*, Berkeley, Los Angeles, and London.

Locke, John, *An Essay Concerning Human Understanding*, ed. P. H. Nidditch, Book II, Chapter XXVII, Oxford, 1975. Reprinted in Perry 1975a.

Mackay, D. M., and Valerie Mackay 1982: 'Explicit Dialogue between Left and Right Half-Systems of Split Brains', *Nature*, 295, pp. 690–1.

Mackie, John 1976: *Problems from Locke*, Oxford, chapter 6.

Nagel, Thomas 1979: 'Brain Bisection and the Unity of Consciousness', in Nagel, *Mortal Questions*, Cambridge. Also reprinted in Perry 1975a.

Nozick, Robert 1981: *Philosophical Explanations*, chapter I, Cambridge, Mass.

Parfit, Derek 1971a: 'On the Importance of Self-Identity', *Journal of Philosophy*, 68, pp. 683–90.

Parfit, Derek 1971b: 'Personal Identity', *The Philosophical Review*, 80, pp. 3–27. Reprinted in Perry 1975a.

Perry, John 1970: 'The Same F', *The Philosophical Review*, 79, pp. 181–200.

Perry, John 1972: 'Can the Self Divide?', *Journal of Philosophy*, 69, pp. 463–88.

Perry, John (ed.) 1975a: *Personal Identity*, Berkeley, Los Angeles, and London.

Perry, John 1975b: 'The Problem of Personal Identity', in Perry 1975a.

Perry, John 1976a: 'The Importance of Being Identical', In Amélie Rorty (ed.), *The Identities of Persons*, Berkeley, Los Angeles, and London.

Perry, John 1976b: Review of Bernard Williams, *Problems of the Self*, *Journal of Philosophy*, 73, pp. 416–28.

Perry, John 1977: 'Frege on Demonstratives', *The Philosophical Review*, 86, pp. 474–97.

Perry, John 1979: 'The Essential Indexical', *Noûs*, 13, pp. 3–21.

Plato, *Phædo*.

Plato, *Timæus*.

Putnam, Hilary 1975: 'The Nature of Mental States', in Putnam, *Mind, Language and Reality, Philosophical Papers, Volume 2*, London.

Quinton, Anthony 1962: 'The Soul', *Journal of Philosophy*, 59, pp. 393–403. Reprinted in Perry 1975a.

Reid, Thomas, *Essays on the Intellectual Powers of Man*, Essay III, chapters 4 and 6. Reprinted in Perry 1975a.

Rorty, Amélie (ed.) 1976: *The Identities of Persons*, Berkeley, Los Angeles, and London.

Russell, Bertrand, 'The Philosophy of Logical Atomism', in R. C. Marsh (ed.), *Logic and Knowledge*, London, 1956.

Salmon, Nathan 1981: *Reference and Essence*, Princeton, and Oxford.

Shoemaker, Sydney 1963: *Self-Knowledge and Self-Identity*, Ithaca, NY.

Shoemaker, Sydney 1968: 'Self-Reference and Self-Awareness', *Journal of Philosophy*, 65, p. 555–67.

Shoemaker, Sydney 1970a: 'Persons and their Pasts', *American Philosophical Quarterly*, 7, pp. 269–85.

Shoemaker, Sydney 1970b: 'Wiggins on Identity', *The Philosophical Review*, 79, pp. 529–44.

Shoemaker, Sydney 1979: 'Identity, Properties and Causality', *Midwest Studies in Philosophy*, No. 4, pp. 321–42.

Shoemaker, Sydney 1982: 'Some Varieties of Functionalism', in J. I. Biro and Robert W. Shahan (eds), *Mind, Brain and Function*, Norman, Oklahoma.

Shoemaker, Sydney 1983: 'On an Argument for Dualism', in C. Ginet and S. Shoemaker (eds), *Knowledge and Mind*, Oxford.

Sklar, Lawrence 1980: 'Semantic Analogy', *Philosophical Studies*, 38, pp. 217–34.

Smart, Brian 1977: 'How can Persons be Ascribed M-Predicates?' *Mind*, 86, pp. 49–66.

Stroud, Barry 1977: *Hume*, London.

Swinburne, Richard 1973–74: 'Personal Identity', *Proceedings of the Aristotelian Society*, 74, pp. 231–48.

Swinburne, Richard 1979: *The Existence of God*, Oxford.

Swinburne, Richard 1981a: *Faith and Reason*, Oxford.

Swinburne, Richard 1981b: *Space and Time*, second edition,

London.

Swinburne, Richard 1983: 'Verificationism and Theories of Space-Time', in Swinburne (ed.), *Space, Time and Causality*, Dordrecht.

Wiggins, David 1967: *Identity and Spatio-temporal Continuity*, Oxford.

Wiggins, David 1980: *Sameness and Substance*, Oxford.

Williams, Bernard 1956–57: 'Personal Identity and Individuation', *Proceedings of the Aristotelian Society*, 57, pp. 229–52. Reprinted in Williams 1973.

Williams, Bernard 1970: 'The Self and the Future', *The Philosophical Review*, 79, pp. 161–80. Reprinted in Williams 1973 and Perry 1975a.

Williams, Bernard 1973: *Problems of the Self*, Cambridge.

Wittgenstein, Ludwig, *The Blue and Brown Books*, Oxford, 1958.

Wittgenstein, Ludwig, *On Certainty*, Oxford, 1979.

Index of Names